THE DAY OF THE CONFEDERACY

ABRAHAM LINCOLN EDITION

∴

VOLUME 30

THE CHRONICLES
OF AMERICA SERIES
ALLEN JOHNSON
EDITOR

GERHARD R. LOMER
CHARLES W. JEFFERYS
ASSISTANT EDITORS

THE DAY OF
THE CONFEDERACY

A CHRONICLE OF THE
EMBATTLED SOUTH
BY NATHANIEL W. STEPHENSON

NEW HAVEN: YALE UNIVERSITY PRESS
TORONTO: GLASGOW, BROOK & CO.
LONDON: HUMPHREY MILFORD
OXFORD UNIVERSITY PRESS

1919

TO

HENRY KENNON DUNHAM

CONTENTS

ILLUSTRATIONS

THE DAY OF THE CONFEDERACY

∴

CHAPTER I

THE SECESSION MOVEMENT

THE secession movement had three distinct stages. The first, beginning with the news that Lincoln was elected, closed with the news, sent broadcast over the South from Charleston, that Federal troops had taken possession of Fort Sumter on the night of the 26th of December. During this period the likelihood of secession was the topic of discussion in the lower South. What to do in case the lower South seceded was the question which perplexed the upper South. In this period no State north of South Carolina contemplated taking the initiative. In the Southeastern and Gulf States immediate action of some sort was expected. Whether it would be secession or some other new course was not certain on the day of Lincoln's election.

Various States earlier in the year had provided for conventions of their people in the event of a Republican victory. The first to assemble was the convention of South Carolina, which organized at Columbia, on December 17, 1860. Two weeks earlier Congress had met. Northerners and Southerners had at once joined issue on their relation in the Union. The House had appointed its committee of thirty-three to consider the condition of the country. So unpromising indeed from the Southern point of view had been the early discussions of this committee that a conference of Southern members of Congress had sent out their famous address *To Our Constituents:* "The argument is exhausted. All hope of relief in the Union . . . is extinguished, and we trust the South will not be deceived by appearances or the pretense of new guarantees. In our judgment the Republicans are resolute in the purpose to grant nothing that will or ought to satisfy the South. We are satisfied the honor, safety, and independence of the Southern people require the organization of a Southern Confederacy — a result to be obtained only by separate state secession." Among the signers of this address were the two statesmen who had in native talent no superiors at Washington —

Judah P. Benjamin of Louisiana and Jefferson Davis of Mississippi.

The appeal *To Our Constituents* was not the only assurance of support tendered to the convention of South Carolina. To represent them at this convention the governors of Alabama and Mississippi had appointed delegates. Mr. Hooker of Mississippi and Mr. Elmore of Alabama made addresses before the convention on the night of the 17th of December. Both reiterated views which during two days of lobbying they had disseminated in Columbia "on all proper occasions." Their argument, summed up in Elmore's report to Governor Moore of Alabama, was "that the only course to unite the Southern States in any plan of coöperation which could promise safety was for South Carolina to take the lead and secede at once without delay or hesitation . . . that the only effective plan of coöperation must ensue after one State had seceded and presented the issue when the plain question would be presented to the other Southern States whether they would stand by the seceding State engaged in a common cause or abandon her to the fate of coercion by the arms of the Government of the United States."

Ten years before, in the unsuccessful secession

movement of 1850 and 1851, Andrew Pickens Butler, perhaps the ablest South Carolinian then living, strove to arrest the movement by exactly the opposite argument. Though desiring secession, he threw all his weight against it because the rest of the South was averse. He charged his opponents, whose leader was Robert Barnwell Rhett, with aiming to place the other Southern States "in such circumstances that, having a common destiny, they would be compelled to be involved in a common sacrifice." He protested that "to force a sovereign State to take a position against its consent is to make of it a reluctant associate. . . . Both interest and honor must require the Southern States to take council together."

That acute thinker was now in his grave. The bold enthusiast whom he defeated in 1851 had now no opponent that was his match. No great personality resisted the fiery advocates from Alabama and Mississippi. Their advice was accepted. On December 20, 1860, the cause that ten years before had failed was successful. The convention, having adjourned from Columbia to Charleston, passed an ordinance of secession.

Meanwhile, in Georgia, at a hundred meetings, the secession issue was being hotly discussed. But there was not yet any certainty which way the scale would turn. An invitation from South Carolina to join in a general Southern convention had been declined by the Governor in November. Governor Brown has left an account ascribing the comparative coolness and deliberation of the hour to the prevailing impression that President Buchanan had pledged himself not to alter the military status at Charleston. In an interview between South Carolina representatives and the President, the Carolinians understood that such a pledge was given. "It was generally understood by the country," says Governor Brown, "that such an agreement . . . had been entered into . . . and that Governor Floyd of Virginia, then Secretary of War, had expressed his determination to resign his position in the Cabinet in case of the refusal of the President to carry out the agreement in good faith. The resignation of Governor Floyd was therefore naturally looked upon, should it occur, as a signal given to the South that reinforcements were to be sent to Charleston and that the coercive policy had been adopted by the Federal Government."

While the "canvass in Georgia for members of the State convention was progressing with much interest on both sides," there came suddenly the news that Anderson had transferred his garrison from Fort Moultrie to the island fortress of Sumter. That same day commissioners from South Carolina, newly arrived at Washington, sought in vain to persuade the President to order Anderson back to Moultrie. The Secretary of War made the subject an issue before the Cabinet. Unable to carry his point, two days later he resigned.[1]

The Georgia Governor, who had not hitherto been in the front rank of the aggressives, now struck a great blow. Senator Toombs had telegraphed from Washington that Fort Pulaski, guarding the Savannah River, was "in danger." The Governor had reached the same conclusion. He mustered the state militia and seized Fort Pulaski. Early in the morning on January 3, 1861, the fort was occupied by Georgia troops. Shortly afterward, Brown wrote to a commissioner sent by the Governor of Alabama to confer with him: "While many of our most patriotic and intelligent citizens in both States have doubted the propriety of immediate secession, I feel quite confident that recent events have dispelled those doubts from the

[1] The President had already asked for Floyd's resignation because of financial irregularities, and Floyd was shrewd enough to use Anderson's *coup* as an excuse for resigning. See Rhodes, *History of the United States*, vol. II, pp. 225, 236 (note).

minds of most men who have, till within the past few days, honestly sustained them." The first stage of the secession movement was at an end; the second had begun.

A belief that Washington had entered upon a policy of aggression swept the lower South. The state conventions assembling about this time passed ordinances of secession — Mississippi, January 9; Florida, January 10; Alabama, January 11; Georgia, January 19; Louisiana, January 26; Texas, February 1. But this result was not achieved without considerable opposition. In Georgia the Unionists put up a stout fight. The issue was not upon the right to secede — virtually no one denied the right — but upon the wisdom of invoking the right. Stephens, gloomy and pessimistic, led the opposition. Toombs came down from Washington to take part with the secessionists. From South Carolina and Alabama, both ceaselessly active for secession, commissioners appeared to lobby at Milledgeville, as commissioners of Alabama and Mississippi had lobbied at Columbia. Besides the out-and-out Unionists, there were those who wanted to temporize, to threaten the North, and to wait for developments. The motion on which these men and the Unionists made their last stand together went against them 164 to 133. Then at last came the square question: Shall we secede? Even on this question, the minority was dangerously large. Though the temporizers came over to the secessionists, and with them came Stephens, there was still a minority of 89 irreconcilables against the majority numbering 208.

"My allegiance," said Stephens afterwards, "was, as I considered it, not due to the United States, or to the people of the United States, but to Georgia, in her sovereign capacity. Georgia had never parted with her right to demand the ultimate allegiance of her citizens."

The attempt in Georgia to restrain impetuosity and advance with deliberation was paralleled in Alabama, where also the aggressives were determined not to permit delay. In the Alabama convention, the conservatives brought forward a plan for a general Southern convention to be held at Nashville in February. It was rejected by a vote of 54 to 45. An attempt to delay secession until after the 4th of March was defeated by the same vote.

The determination of the radicals to precipitate the issue received interesting criticism from the Governor of Texas, old Sam Houston. To a

ALEXANDER H. STEPHENS

Photograph by Brady. In the collection of L. C. Handy, Washington.

ALEXANDER H. STEPHENS

Photograph by Brady. In the collection of L. C. Handy, Washington.

commissioner from Alabama who was sent out to preach the cause in Texas the Governor wrote, in substance, that since Alabama would not wait to consult the people of Texas he saw nothing to discuss at that time, and he went on to say:

Recognizing as I do the fact that the sectional tendencies of the Black Republican party call for determined constitutional resistance at the hands of the united South, I also feel that the million and a half of noble-hearted, conservative men who have stood by the South, even to this hour, deserve some sympathy and support. Although we have lost the day, we have to recollect that our conservative Northern friends cast over a quarter of a million more votes against the Black Republicans than we of the entire South. I cannot declare myself ready to desert them as well as our Southern brethren of the border (and such, I believe, will be the sentiment of Texas) until at least one firm attempt has been made to preserve our constitutional rights within the Union.

Nevertheless, Houston was not able to control his State. Delegates from Texas attended the later sessions of a general Congress of the seceding States which, on the invitation of Alabama, met at Montgomery on the 4th of February. A contemporary document of singular interest today is the series of resolutions adopted by the Legislature of North Carolina, setting forth that, as the

State was a member of the Federal Union, it could not accept the invitation of Alabama but should send delegates for the purpose of persuading the South to effect a readjustment on the basis of the Crittenden Compromise as modified by the Legislature of Virginia. The commissioners were sent, were graciously received, were accorded seats in the Congress, but they exerted no influence on the course of its action.

The Congress speedily organized a provisional Government for the Confederate States of America. The Constitution of the United States, rather hastily reconsidered, became with a few inevitable alterations the Constitution of the Confederacy.[1]

---

[1] To the observer of a later age this document appears a thing of haste. Like the framers of the Constitution of 1787, who omitted from their document some principles which they took for granted, the framers of 1861 left unstated their most distinctive views. The basal idea upon which the revolution proceeded, the right of secession, is not to be found in the new Constitution. Though the preamble declares that the States are acting in their sovereign and independent character, the new Confederation is declared "permanent." In the body of the document are provisions similar to those in the Federal Constitution enabling a majority of two-thirds of the States to amend at their pleasure, thus imposing their will upon the minority. With three notable exceptions the new Constitution, subsequent to the preamble, does little more than restate the Constitution of 1787 re-arranged so as to include those basal principles of the English law added to the earlier Constitution by the first eight amendments. The three exceptions are the prohibitions (1) of the payment of bounties, (2) of the levying of duties to promote any one form of industry, and

Davis was unanimously elected President; Stephens, Vice-President. Provision was made for raising an army. Commissioners were dispatched to Washington to negotiate a treaty with the United States; other commissioners were sent to Virginia to attempt to withdraw that great commonwealth from the Union.

The upper South was thus placed in a painful situation. Its sympathies were with the seceding States. Most of its people felt also that if coercion was attempted, the issue would become for Virginia and North Carolina, no less than for South Carolina and Alabama, simply a matter of self-preservation. As early as January, in the exciting days when Floyd's resignation was being interpreted as a call to arms, the Virginia Legislature had resolved that it would not consent to the coercion of a seceding State. In May the Speaker of the North Carolina Legislature assured a commissioner from Georgia that North Carolina would never consent to the movement of troops "from or

(3) of appropriations for internal improvements. Here was a monument to the battle over these matters in the Federal Congress. As to the mechanism of the new Government it was the same as the old except for a few changes of detail. The presidential term was lengthened to six years and the President was forbidden to succeed himself. The President was given the power to veto items in appropriation bills. The African slave-trade was prohibited.

across" the State to attack a seceding State. But neither Virginia nor North Carolina in this second stage of the movement wanted to secede. They wanted to preserve the Union, but along with the Union they wanted the principle of local autonomy. It was a period of tense anxiety in those States of the upper South. The frame of mind of the men who loved the Union but who loved equally their own States and were firm for local autonomy is summed up in a letter in which Mrs. Robert E. Lee describes the anguish of her husband as he confronted the possibility of a divided country.

The real tragedy of the time lay in the failure of the advocates of these two great principles — each so necessary to a far-flung democratic country in a world of great powers! — the failure to coördinate them so as to insure freedom at home and strength abroad. The principle for which Lincoln stood has saved Americans in the Great War from playing such a trembling part as that of Holland. The principle which seemed to Lee even more essential, which did not perish at Appomattox but was transformed and not destroyed, is what has kept us from becoming a western Prussia. And yet if only it had been possible to coördinate the two without the price of war! It was not possible because of the stored up bitterness of a quarter century of recrimination. But Virginia made a last desperate attempt to preserve the Union by calling the Peace Convention. It assembled at Washington the day the Confederate Congress met at Montgomery. Though twenty-one States sent delegates, it was no more able to effect a working scheme of compromise than was the House committee of thirty-three or the Senate committee of thirteen, both of which had striven, had failed, and had gone their ways to a place in the great company of historic futilities.

And so the Peace Convention came and went, and there was no consolation for the troubled men of the upper South who did not want to secede but were resolved not to abandon local autonomy. Virginia was the key to the situation. If Virginia could be forced into secession, the rest of the upper South would inevitably follow. Therefore a Virginia hothead, Roger A. Pryor, being in Charleston in those wavering days, poured out his heart in fiery words, urging a Charleston crowd to precipitate war, in the certainty that Virginia would then have to come to their aid. When at last Sumter was fired upon and Lincoln called for volunteers, the second stage of the secession movement ended in a thunderclap. The third period was occupied by the second group of secessions: Virginia on the 17th of April, North Carolina and Arkansas during May, Tennessee early in June.

Sumter was the turning-point. The boom of the first cannon trained on the island fortress deserves all the rhetoric it has inspired. Who was immediately responsible for that firing which was destiny? Ultimate responsibility is not upon any person. War had to be. If Sumter had not been the starting-point, some other would have been found. Nevertheless the question of immediate responsibility, of whose word it was that served as the signal to begin, has produced an historic controversy.

When it was known at Charleston that Lincoln would attempt to provision the fort, the South Carolina authorities referred the matter to the Confederate authorities. The Cabinet, in a fateful session at Montgomery, hesitated — drawn between the wish to keep their hold upon the moderates of the North, who were trying to stave off war, and the desire to precipitate Virginia into the lists. Toombs, Secretary of State in the new Government, wavered; then seemed to find his resolution and came out strong against a demand for

ROBERT TOOMBS

Photograph by H. P. Cook, Richmond, Virginia.

ROBERT TOOMBS

Photograph by H. P. Cook, Richmond, Virginia.

Enuvure, Anderson-Lamb Co. N.Y.

surrender. "It is suicide, murder, and will lose us every friend at the North. . . . It is unnecessary; it puts us in the wrong; it is fatal," said he. But the Cabinet and the President decided to take the risk. To General Pierre Beauregard, recently placed in command of the militia assembled at Charleston, word was sent to demand the surrender of Fort Sumter.

On Thursday, the 7th of April, besides his instructions from Montgomery, Beauregard was in receipt of a telegram from the Confederate commissioners at Washington, repeating newspaper statements that the Federal relief expedition intended to land a force "which will overcome all opposition." There seems no doubt that Beauregard did not believe that the expedition was intended merely to provision Sumter. Probably every one in Charleston thought that the Federal authorities were trying to deceive them, that Lincoln's promise not to do more than provision Sumter was a mere blind. Fearfulness that delay might render Sumter impregnable lay back of Beauregard's formal demand, on the 11th of April, for the surrender of the fort. Anderson refused but "made some verbal observations" to the aides who brought him the demand. In effect he said that lack of supplies would compel him to surrender by the fifteenth. When this information was taken back to the city, eager crowds were in the streets of Charleston discussing the report that a bombardment would soon begin. But the afternoon passed; night fell; and nothing was done. On the beautiful terrace along the sea known as East Battery, people congregated, watching the silent fortress whose brick walls rose sheer from the midst of the harbor. The early hours of the night went by and as midnight approached and still there was no flash from either the fortress or the shore batteries which threatened it, the crowds broke up.

Meanwhile there was anxious consultation at the hotel where Beauregard had fixed his headquarters. Pilots came in from the sea to report to the General that a Federal vessel had appeared off the mouth of the harbor. This news may well explain the hasty dispatch of a second expedition to Sumter in the middle of the night. At half after one, Friday morning, four young men, aides of Beauregard, entered the fort. Anderson repeated his refusal to surrender at once but admitted that he would have to surrender within three days. Thereupon the aides held a council of war. They decided that the reply was unsatisfactory and wrote out a brief note which they handed to Anderson informing him that the Confederates would open "fire upon Fort Sumter in one hour from this time." The note was dated 3:20 A.M. The aides then proceeded to Fort Johnston on the south side of the harbor and gave the order to fire.

The council of the aides at Sumter is the dramatic detail that has caught the imagination of historians and has led them, at least in some cases, to yield to a literary temptation. It is so dramatic — that scene of the four young men holding in their hands, during a moment of absolute destiny, the fate of a people; four young men, in the irresponsible ardor of youth, refusing to wait three days and forcing war at the instant! It is so dramatic that one cannot judge harshly the artistic temper which is unable to reject it. But is the incident historic? Did the four young men come to Sumter without definite instructions? Was their conference really anything more than a careful comparing of notes to make sure they were doing what they were intended to do? Is not the real clue to the event a message from Beauregard to the Secretary of War telling of his interview with the pilots?[1]

---

[1] A chief authority for the dramatic version of the council of the aides is that fiery Virginian, Roger A. Pryor. He and another accom-

Dawn was breaking gray, with a faint rain in the air, when the first boom of the cannon awakened the city. Other detonations followed in quick succession. Shells rose into the night from both sides of the harbor and from floating batteries. How lightly Charleston slept that night may be inferred from the accounts in the newspapers. "At the report of the first gun," says the *Courier*, "the city was nearly emptied of its inhabitants who crowded the Battery and the wharves to witness the conflict."

The East Battery and the lower harbor of the lovely city of Charleston have been preserved almost without alteration. What they are today they were in the breaking dawn on April 12, 1861. Business has gone up the rivers between which Charleston lies and has left the point of the city's peninsula, where East Battery looks outward to the Atlantic, in its perfect charm. There large houses, pillared, with high piazzas, stand apart one from another among gardens. With few exceptions they

---

panied the official messengers, the signers of the note to Anderson, James Chestnut and Stephen Lee. Years afterwards Pryor told the story of the council in a way to establish its dramatic significance. But would there be anything strange if a veteran survivor, looking back to his youth, as all of us do through more or less of mirage, yielded to the unconscious artist that is in us all and dramatized this event unaware?

were built before the middle of the century and all, with one exception, show the classical taste of those days. The mariner, entering the spacious inner sea that is Charleston Harbor, sights this row of stately mansions even before he crosses the bar seven miles distant. Holding straight onward up into the land he heads first for the famous little island where, nowadays, in their halo of thrilling recollection, the walls of Sumter, rising sheer from the bosom of the water, drowse idle. Close under the lee of Sumter, the incoming steersman brings his ship about and chooses, probably, the eastward of two huge tentacles of the sea between which lies the city's long but narrow peninsula. To the steersman it shows a skyline serrated by steeples, fronted by sea, flanked southward by sea, backgrounded by an estuary, and looped about by a sickle of wooded islands.

This same scene, so far as city and nature go, was beheld by the crowds that swarmed East Battery, a flagstone marine parade along the seaward side of the boulevard that faces Sumter; that filled the windows and even the housetops; that watched the bombardment with the eagerness of an audience in an amphitheater; that applauded every telling shot with clapping of hands and waving of shawls and handkerchiefs. The fort lay distant from them about three miles, but only some fifteen hundred yards from Fort Johnston on one side and about a mile from Fort Moultrie on the other. From both of these latter, the cannon of those days were equal to the task of harassing Sumter. Early in the morning of the 12th of April, though not until broad day had come, did Anderson make reply. All that day, at first under heavily rolling cloud and later through curiously misty sunshine, the fire and counterfire continued. "The enthusiasm and fearlessness of the spectators," says the Charleston *Mercury*, "knew no bounds." Reckless observers even put out in small boats and roamed about the harbor almost under the guns of the fort. Outside the bar, vessels of the relieving squadron were now visible, and to these Anderson signaled for aid. They made an attempt to reach the fort, but only part of the squadron had arrived, and the vessels necessary to raise the siege were not there. The attempt ended in failure. When night came, a string of rowboats each carrying a huge torch kept watch along the bar to guard against surprise from the sea.

On that Friday night the harbor was swept by

storm. But in spite of torrents of rain East Battery and the rooftops were thronged. "The wind was inshore and the booming was startlingly distinct." At the height of the bombardment, the sky above Sumter seemed to be filled with the flashes of bursting shells. But during this wild night Sumter itself was both dark and silent. Its casements did not have adequate lamps and the guns could not be used except by day. When morning broke, clear and bright after the night's storm, the duel was resumed.

The walls of Sumter were now crumbling. At eight o'clock Saturday morning the barracks took fire. Soon after it was perceived from the shore that the flag was down. Beauregard at once sent offers of assistance. With Sumter in flames above his head, Anderson replied that he had not surrendered; he declined assistance; and he hauled up his flag. Later in the day the flagstaff was shot in two and again the flag fell, and again it was raised. Flames had been kindled anew by red-hot shot, and now the magazine was in danger. Quantities of powder were thrown into the sea. Still the rain of red-hot shot continued. About noon, Saturday, says the *Courier*, "flames burst out from every quarter of Sumter and poured from many

of its portholes . . . the wind was from the west
driving the smoke across the fort into the em-
brasures where the gunners were at work." Nevertheless, "as if served with a new impulse," the
guns of Sumter redoubled their fire. But it was
not in human endurance to keep on in the midst
of the burning fort. This splendid last effort was
short. At a quarter after one, Anderson ceased
firing and raised a white flag. Negotiations followed ending in terms of surrender — Anderson to
be allowed to remove his garrison to the fleet lying
idle beyond the bar and to salute the flag of the
United States before taking it down. The bombardment had lasted thirty-two hours without a
death on either side. The evacuation of the fort
was to take place next day.

The afternoon of Sunday, the 14th of April, was
a gala day in the harbor of Charleston. The sun-
light slanted across the roofs of the city, sparkled
upon the sea. Deep and rich the harbor always
looks in the spring sunshine on bright afternoons.
The filmy atmosphere of these latitudes, at that
time of year, makes the sky above the darkling,
afternoon sea a pale but luminous turquoise.
There is a wonderful soft strength in the peaceful
brightness of the sun. In such an atmosphere the

harbor was flecked with brilliantly decked craft of every description, all in a flutter of flags and carrying a host of passengers in gala dress. The city swarmed across the water to witness the ceremony of evacuation. Wherry men did a thriving business carrying passengers to the fort.

Anderson withdrew from Sumter shortly after two o'clock amid a salute of fifty guns. The Confederates took possession. At half after four a new flag was raised above the battered and fire-swept walls.

CHAPTER II

It has never been explained why Jefferson Davis was chosen President of the Confederacy. He did not seek the office and did not wish it. He dreamed of high military command. As a study in the irony of fate, Davis's career is made to the hand of the dramatist. An instinctive soldier, he was driven by circumstances three times to renounce the profession of arms for a less congenial civilian life. His final renunciation, which proved to be of the nature of tragedy, was his acceptance of the office of President. Indeed, why the office was given to him seems a mystery. Rhett was a more logical candidate. And when Rhett, early in the lobbying at Montgomery, was set aside as too much of a radical, Toombs seemed for a time the certain choice of the majority. The change to Davis came suddenly at the last moment. It was puzzling at the time; it is puzzling still.

24

Rhett, though doubtless bitterly disappointed, bore himself with the *savoir faire* of a great gentleman. At the inauguration, it was on Rhett's arm that Davis leaned as he entered the hall of the Confederate Congress. The night before, in a public address, Yancey had said that the man and the hour were met. The story of the Confederacy is filled with dramatic moments, but to the thoughtful observer few are more dramatic than the conjunction of these three men in the inauguration of the Confederate President. Beneath a surface of apparent unanimity they carried, like concealed weapons, points of view that were in deadly antagonism. This antagonism had not revealed itself hitherto. It was destined to reveal itself almost immediately. It went so deep and spread so far that unless we understand it, the Confederate story will be unintelligible.

A strange fatality destined all three of these great men to despair. Yancey, who was perhaps most directly answerable of the three for the existence of the Confederacy, lost influence almost from the moment when his dream became established. Davis was partly responsible, for he promptly sent him out of the country on the bootless English mission. Thereafter, until his death in 1863,

Yancey was a waning, overshadowed figure, steadily lapsing into the background. It may be that those critics are right who say he was only an agitator. The day of the mere agitator was gone. Yancey passed rapidly into futile but bitter antagonism to Davis. In this attitude he was soon to be matched by Rhett.

The discontent of the Rhett faction because their leader was not given the portfolio of the State Department found immediate voice. But the conclusion drawn by some that Rhett's subsequent course sprang from personal vindictiveness is trifling. He was too large a personality, too well defined an intellect, to be thus explained. Very probably Davis made his first great blunder in failing to propitiate the Rhett faction. And yet few things are more certain than that the two men, the two factions which they symbolized, could not have formed a permanent alliance. Had Rhett entered the Cabinet he could not have remained in it consistently for any considerable time. The measures in which, presently, the Administration showed its hand were measures in which Rhett could not acquiesce. From the start he was predestined to his eventual position — the great, unavailing genius of the opposition.

As to the comparative ignoring of these leaders of secession by the Government which secession had created, it is often said that the explanation is to be found in a generous as well as politic desire to put in office the moderates and even the conservatives. Davis, relatively, was a moderate. Stephens was a conservative. Many of the most pronounced opponents of secession were given places in the public service. Toombs, who received the portfolio of State, though a secessionist, was conspicuously a moderate when compared with Rhett and Yancey. The adroit Benjamin, who became Attorney-General, had few points in common with the great extremists of Alabama and South Carolina.

However, the dictum that the personnel of the new Government was a triumph for conservatism over radicalism signifies little. There was a division among Southerners which scarcely any of them had realized except briefly in the premature battle over secession in 1851. It was the division between those who were conscious of the region as a whole and those who were not. Explain it as you will, there was a moment just after the secession movement succeeded when the South seemed to realize itself as a whole, when it turned intuitively to those men who, as time was to demonstrate, shared this realization. For the moment it turned away from those others, however great their part in secession, who lacked this sense of unity.

At this point, geography becomes essential. The South fell, institutionally, into two grand divisions: one, with an old and firmly established social order, where consciousness of the locality went back to remote times; another, newly settled, where conditions were still fluid, where that sense of the sacredness of local institutions had not yet formed.

A typical community of the first-named class was South Carolina. Her people had to a remarkable degree been rendered state-conscious partly by their geographical neighbors, and partly by their long and illustrious history, which had been interwoven with great European interests during the colonial era and with great national interests under the Republic. It is possible also that the Huguenots, though few in numbers, had exercised upon the State a subtle and pervasive influence through their intellectual power and their Latin sense for institutions.

In South Carolina, too, a wealthy leisure class with a passion for affairs had cultivated enthusi-

astically that fine art which is the pride of all
aristocratic societies, the service of the State as a
profession high and exclusive, free from vulgar
taint. In South Carolina all things conspired to
uphold and strengthen the sense of the State as an
object of veneration, as something over and above
the mere social order, as the sacred embodiment
of the ideals of the community. Thus it is fair to
say that what has animated the heroic little countries of the Old World — Switzerland and Serbia
and ever-glorious Belgium — with their passion
to remain themselves, animated South Carolina in
1861. Just as Serbia was willing to fight to the
death rather than merge her identity in the mosaic
of the Austrian Empire, so this little American
community saw nothing of happiness in any future
that did not secure its virtual independence.

Typical of the newer order in the South was the
community that formed the President of the Confederacy. In the history of Mississippi previous to
the war there are six great names — Jacob Thompson, John A. Quitman, Henry S. Foote, Robert J.
Walker, Sergeant S. Prentiss, and Jefferson Davis.
Not one of them was born in the State. Thompson was born in North Carolina; Quitman in New
York; Foote in Virginia; Walker in Pennsylvania;

Prentiss in Maine; Davis in Kentucky. In 1861 the State was but forty-four years old, younger than its most illustrious sons — if the paradox may be permitted. How could they think of it as an entity existing in itself, antedating not only themselves but their traditions, circumscribing them with its all-embracing, indisputable reality? These men spoke the language of state rights. It is true that in politics, combating the North, they used the political philosophy taught them by South Carolina. But it was a mental weapon in political debate; it was not for them an emotional fact.

And yet these men of the Southwest had an ideal of their own as vivid and as binding as the state ideal of the men of the eastern coast. Though half their leaders were born in the North, the people themselves were overwhelmingly Southern. From all the older States, all round the huge crescent which swung around from Kentucky coastwise to Florida, immigration in the twenties and thirties had poured into Mississippi. Consequently the new community presented a composite picture of the whole South, and like all composite pictures it emphasized only the factors common to all its parts. What all the South had in common, what made a man a Southerner in the general sense —

in distinction from a Northerner on the one hand,
or a Virginian, Carolinian, Georgian, on the other
— could have been observed with clearness in
Mississippi, just before the war, as nowhere else.
Therefore, the fulfillment of the ideal of Southern life in general terms was the vision of things
hoped for by the new men of the Southwest. The
features of that vision were common to them all —
country life, broad acres, generous hospitality, an
aristocratic system. The temperaments of these
men were sufficiently buoyant to enable them to
apprehend this ideal even before it had materi-
alized. Their romantic minds could see the gold at
the end of the rainbow. Theirs was not the pride
of administering a well-ordered, inherited system,
but the joy of building a new system, in their minds
wholly elastic, to be sure, but still inspired by that
old system.

What may be called the sense of Southern
nationality as opposed to the sense of state rights,
strictly speaking, distinguished this brilliant young
community of the Southwest. In that community
Davis spent the years that appear to have been the
most impressionable of his life. Belonging to a
"new" family just emerging into wealth, he began
life as a West Pointer and saw gallant service as a

youth on the frontier; resigned from the army to pursue a romantic attachment; came home to lead the life of a wealthy planter and receive the impress of Mississippi; made his entry into politics, still a soldier at heart, with the philosophy of state rights on his lips, but in his heart that sense of the Southern people as a new nation, which needed only the occasion to make it the relentless enemy of the rights of the individual Southern States. Add together the instinctive military point of view and this Southern nationalism that even in 1861 had scarcely revealed itself; join with these a fearless and haughty spirit, proud to the verge of arrogance, but perfectly devoted, perfectly sincere; and you have the main lines of the political character of Davis when he became President. It may be that as he went forward in his great undertaking, as antagonisms developed, as Rhett and others turned against him, Davis hardened. He lost whatever comprehension he once had of the Rhett type. Seeking to weld into one irresistible unit all the military power of the South, he became at last in the eyes of his opponents a monster, while to him, more and more positively, the others became mere dreamers.

It took about a year for this irrepressible

conflict within the Confederacy to reveal itself. During the twelve months following Davis's election as provisional President, he dominated the situation, though the Charleston *Mercury*, the Rhett organ, found opportunities to be sharply critical of the President. He assembled armies; he initiated heroic efforts to make up for the handicap of the South in the manufacture of munitions and succeeded in starting a number of munition plants; though powerless to prevent the establishment of the blockade, he was able during that first year to keep in touch with Europe, to start out Confederate privateers upon the high seas, and to import a considerable quantity of arms and supplies. At the close of the year the Confederate armies were approaching general efficiency, for all their enormous handicap, almost if not quite as rapidly as were the Union armies. And the one great event of the year on land, the first battle of Manassas, or Bull Run, was a signal Confederate victory.

To be sure Davis was severely criticized in some quarters for not adopting an aggressive policy. The Confederate Government, whether wisely or foolishly, had not taken the people into its confidence and the lack of munitions was not generally appreciated. The easy popular cries were all sounded: "We are standing still!" "The country is being invaded!" "The President is a do-nothing!" From the coast regions especially, where the blockade was felt in all its severity, the outcry was loud.

Nevertheless, the South in the main was content with the Administration during most of the first year. In November, when the general elections were held, Davis was chosen without opposition as the first regular Confederate President for six years, and Stephens became the Vice-President. The election was followed by an important change in the Southern Cabinet. Benjamin became Secretary of War, in succession to the first War Secretary, Leroy P. Walker. Toombs had already left the Confederate Cabinet. Complaining that Davis degraded him to the level of a mere clerk, he had withdrawn the previous July. His successor in the State Department was R. M. T. Hunter of Virginia, who remained in office until February, 1862, when his removal to the Confederate Senate opened the way for a further advancement of Benjamin.

Richmond, which had been designated as the capital soon after the secession of Virginia, was the

RESIDENCE OF JEFFERSON DAVIS, RICHMOND, VIRGINIA

Photograph by H. P. Cook, Richmond, Virginia.

RESIDENCE OF JEFFERSON DAVIS, RICHMOND, VIRGINIA

Photograph by H. P. Cook, Richmond, Virginia.

scene of the inauguration, on February 22, 1862. Although the weather proved bleak and rainy, an immense crowd gathered around the Washington monument, in Capitol Square, to listen to the inaugural address. By this time the confidence in the Government, which was felt generally at the time of the election, had suffered a shock. Foreign affairs were not progressing satisfactorily. Though England had accorded to the Confederacy the status of a belligerent, this was poor consolation for her refusal to make full recognition of the new Government as an independent power. Dread of internal distress was increasing. Gold commanded a premium of fifty per cent. Disorder was a feature of the life in the cities. It was known that several recent military events had been victories for the Federals. A rumor was abroad that some great disaster had taken place in Tennessee. The crowd listened anxiously to hear the rumor denied by the President. But it was not denied. The tense listeners noted two sentences which formed an admission that the situation was grave: "A million men, it is estimated, are now standing in hostile array and waging war along a frontier of thousands of miles. Battles have been fought, sieges have been conducted, and although the contest is not ended, and the tide for the moment is against us, the final result in our favor is not doubtful."

Behind these carefully guarded words lay serious alarm, not only with regard to the operations at the front but as to the composition of the army. It had been raised under various laws and its portions were subject to conflicting classifications; it was partly a group of state armies, partly a single Confederate army. None of its members had enlisted for long terms. Many enlistments would expire early in 1862. The fears of the Confederate Administration with regard to this matter, together with its alarm about the events at the front, were expressed by Davis in a frank message to the Southern Congress, three days later. "I have hoped," said he, "for several days to receive official reports in relation to our discomfiture at Roanoke Island and the fall of Fort Donelson. They have not yet reached me. . . . The hope is still entertained that our reported losses at Fort Donelson have been greatly exaggerated. . . ." He went on to condemn the policy of enlistments for short terms, "against which," said he, "I have steadily contended"; and he enlarged upon the danger that even patriotic men, who intended to reënlist, might go home to put their affairs in order and that thus, at a critical moment, the army might be seriously reduced. The accompanying report of the Confederate Secretary of War showed a total in the army of 340,250 men. This was an inadequate force with which to meet the great hosts which were being organized against it in the North. To permit the slightest reduction of the army at that moment seemed to the Southern President suicidal.

But Davis waited some time longer before proposing to the Confederate Congress the adoption of conscription. Meanwhile, the details of two great reverses, the loss of Roanoke Island and the loss of Fort Donelson, became generally known. Apprehension gathered strength. Newspapers began to discuss conscription as something inevitable. At last, on March 28, 1862, Davis sent a message to the Confederate Congress advising the conscription of all white males between the ages of eighteen and thirty-five. For this suggestion Congress was ripe, and the first Conscription Act of the Confederacy was signed by the President on the 16th of April. The age of eligibility was fixed as Davis had advised; the term of service was to be three years; every one then in service was to be retained in service during three years from the date of his original enlistment.

This statute may be thought of as a great victory on the part of the Administration. It was the climax of a policy of centralization in the military establishment to which Davis had committed himself by the veto, in January, of "A bill to authorize the Secretary of War to receive into the service of the Confederate States a regiment of volunteers for the protection of the frontier of Texas." This regiment was to be under the control of the Governor of the State. In refusing to accept such troops, Davis laid down the main proposition upon which he stood as military executive to the end of the war, a proposition which immediately set debate raging: "Unity and cooperation by the troops of all the States are indispensable to success, and I must view with regret this as well as all other indications of a purpose to divide the power of States by dividing the means to be employed in efforts to carry on separate operations."

In these military measures of the early months of 1862 Davis's purpose became clear. He was bent upon instituting a strong government, able to push the war through, and careless of the niceties of constitutional law or of the exact prerogatives of the States. His position was expressed in the course of the year by a Virginia newspaper: "It will be time enough to distract the councils of the State about imaginary violations of constitutional law by the supreme government when our independence is achieved, established, and acknowledged. It will not be until then that the sovereignty of the States will be a reality." But there were many Southerners who could not accept this point of view. The *Mercury* was sharply critical of the veto of the Texas Regiment Bill. In the interval between the Texas veto and the passing of the Conscription Act, the state convention of North Carolina demanded the return of North Carolina volunteers for the defense of their own State. No sooner was the Conscription Act passed than its constitutionality was attacked. As the Confederacy had no Supreme Court, the question came up before state courts. One after another, several state supreme courts pronounced the act constitutional and in most of the States the constitutional issue was gradually allowed to lapse.

Nevertheless, Davis had opened Pandora's box. The clash between State and Confederate authority had begun. An opposition party began to

form. In this first stage of its definite existence,
the opposition made an interesting attempt to
control the Cabinet. Secretary Benjamin, though
greatly trusted by the President, seems never to
have been a popular minister. Congress attempted
to load upon Benjamin the blame for Roanoke
Island and Fort Donelson. In the House a motion
was introduced to the effect that Benjamin had
"not the confidence of the people of the Confederate States nor of the army . . . and that we
most respectfully request his retirement" from the
office of Secretary of War. Friends of the Administration tabled the motion. Davis extricated his
friend by taking advantage of Hunter's retirement
and promoting Benjamin to the State Department.
A month later a congressional committee appointed to investigate the affair of Roanoke Island
exonerated the officer in command and laid the
blame on his superiors, including "the late Secretary of War."

With Benjamin safe in the Department of State,
with the majority in the Confederate Congress
still fairly manageable, with the Conscription Act
in force, Davis seemed to be strong enough in the
spring of 1862 to ignore the gathering opposition.
And yet there was another measure, second only

in the President's eyes to the Conscription Act, that was to breed trouble. This was the first of the series of acts empowering him to suspend the privilege of the writ of *habeas corpus*. Under this act he was permitted to set up martial law in any district threatened with invasion. The cause of this drastic measure was the confusion and the general demoralization that existed wherever the close approach of the enemy created a situation too complex for the ordinary civil authorities. Davis made use of the power thus given to him and proclaimed martial law in Richmond, in Norfolk, in parts of South Carolina, and elsewhere. It was on Richmond that the hand of the Administration fell heaviest. The capital was the center of a great camp; its sudden and vast increase in population had been the signal for all the criminal class near and far to hurry thither in the hope of a new field of spoliation; to deal with this immense human congestion, the local police were powerless; every variety of abominable contrivance to entrap and debauch men for a price was in brazen operation. The first care of the Government under the new law was the cleansing of the capital. General John H. Winder, appointed military governor, did the job with thoroughness. He closed the barrooms, disarmed the populace, and for the time at least swept the city clean of criminals. The Administration also made certain political arrests, and even imprisoned some extreme opponents of the Government for "offenses not enumerated and not cognizable under the regular process of law." Such arrests gave the enemies of the Administration another handle against it. As we shall see later, the use that Davis made of martial law was distorted by a thousand fault-finders and was made the basis of the charge that the President was aiming at absolute power.

At the moment, however, Davis was master of the situation. The six months following April 1, 1862, were doubtless, from his own point of view, the most satisfactory part of his career as Confederate President. These months were indeed filled with peril. There was a time when McClellan's advance up the Peninsula appeared so threatening that the archives of the Government were packed on railway cars prepared for immediate removal should evacuation be necessary. There were the other great disasters during that year, including the loss of New Orleans. The President himself experienced a profound personal sorrow in the death of his friend, Albert Sidney

Johnston, in the bloody fight at Shiloh. It was in the midst of this time that tried men's souls that the Richmond *Examiner* achieved an unenvied immortality for one of its articles on the Administration. At a moment when nothing should have been said to discredit in any way the struggling Government, it described Davis as weak with fear telling his beads in a corner of St. Paul's Church. This paper, along with the Charleston *Mercury*, led the Opposition. Throughout Confederate history these two, which were very ably edited, did the thinking for the enemies of Davis. We shall meet them time and again.

A true picture of Davis would have shown the President resolute and resourceful, at perhaps the height of his powers. He recruited and supplied the armies; he fortified Richmond; he sustained the great captain whom he had placed in command while McClellan was at the gates. When the tide had turned and the Army of the Potomac sullenly withdrew, baffled, there occurred the one brief space in Confederate history that was pure sunshine. In this period took place the splendid victory of Second Manassas. The strong military policy of the Administration had given the Confederacy powerful armies. Lee had inspired them

with victory.   This period of buoyant hope cul-
minated in the great offensive design which followed Second Manassas.   It was known that the
Northern people, or a large part of them, had
suffered a reaction; the tide was setting strong
against the Lincoln Government; in the autumn,
the Northern elections would be held.   To influence those elections and at the same time to
drive the Northern armies back into their own
section; to draw Maryland and Kentucky into the
Confederate States; to fall upon the invaders in
the Southwest and recover the lower Mississippi —
to accomplish all these results was the confident
expectation of the President and his advisers as
they planned their great triple offensive in August,
1862.   Lee was to invade Maryland; Bragg was to
invade Kentucky; Van Dorn was to break the
hold of the Federals in the Southwest.   If there
is one moment that is to be considered the climax
of Davis's career, the high-water mark of Confederate hope, it was the moment of joyous expectation when the triple offensive was launched,
when Lee's army, on a brilliant autumn day,
crossed the Potomac, singing *Maryland, my
Maryland*.

CHAPTER III

THE FALL OF KING COTTON

WHILE the Confederate Executive was building up its military establishment, the Treasury was struggling with the problem of paying for it. The problem was destined to become insoluble. From the vantage-point of a later time we can now see that nothing could have provided a solution short of appropriation and mobilization of the whole industrial power of the country along with the whole military power — a conscription of wealth of every kind together with conscription of men. But in 1862 such an idea was too advanced for any group of Americans. Nor, in that year, was there as yet any certain evidence that the Treasury was facing an impossible situation. Its endeavors were taken lightly — at first, almost gaily — because of the profound illusion which permeated Southern thought that Cotton was King.

Obviously, if the Southern ports could be kept open and cotton could continue to go to market, the Confederate financial problem was not serious. When Davis, soon after his first inauguration, sent Yancey, Rost, and Mann as commissioners to Europe to press the claims of the Confederacy for recognition, very few Southerners had any doubt that the blockade would be short-lived. "Cotton is King" was the answer that silenced all questions. Without American cotton the English mills would have to shut down; the operatives would starve; famine and discontent would between them force the British ministry to intervene in American affairs. There were, indeed, a few far-sighted men who perceived that this confidence was ill-based and that cotton, though it was a power in the financial world, was not the commercial king. The majority of the population, however, had to learn this truth from keen experience.

Several events of 1861 for a time seemed to confirm this illusion. The Queen's proclamation in the spring, giving the Confederacy the status of a belligerent, and, in the autumn, the demand by the British Government for the surrender of the commissioners, Mason and Slidell, who had been taken from a British packet by a Union cruiser —

both these events seemed to indicate active British sympathy. In England, to be sure, Yancey became disillusioned. He saw that the international situation was not so simple as it seemed; that while the South had powerful friends abroad, it also had powerful foes; that the British anti-slavery party was a more formidable enemy than he had expected it to be; and that intervention was not a foregone conclusion. The task of an unrecognized ambassador being too annoying for him, Yancey was relieved at his own request and Mason was sent out to take his place. A singular little incident like a dismal prophecy occurred as Yancey was on his way home. He passed through Havana early in 1862, when the news of the surrender of Fort Donelson had begun to stagger the hopes and impair the prestige of the Confederates. By the advice of the Confederate agent in Cuba, Yancey did not call on the Spanish Governor but sent him word that "delicacy alone prompted his departure without the gratification of a personal interview." The Governor expressed himself as "exceedingly grateful for the noble sentiment which prevented" Yancey from causing international complications at Havana.

The history of the first year of Confederate

foreign affairs is interwoven with the history of Confederate finance. During that year the South became a great buyer in Europe. Arms, powder, cloth, machinery, medicines, ships, a thousand things, had all to be bought abroad. To establish the foreign credit of the new Government was the arduous task of the Confederate Secretary of the Treasury, Christopher G. Memminger. The first great campaign of the war was not fought by armies. It was a commercial campaign fought by agents of the Federal and Confederate governments and having for its aim the cornering of the munitions market in Europe. In this campaign the Federal agents had decisive advantages: their credit was never questioned, and their enormous purchases were never doubtful ventures for the European sellers. In some cases their superior credit enabled them to overbid the Confederate agents and to appropriate large contracts which the Confederates had negotiated but which they could not hold because of the precariousness of their credit. And yet, all things considered, the Confederate agents made a good showing. In the report of the Secretary of War in February, 1862, the number of rifles contracted for abroad was put at 91,000, of which 15,000 had been delivered.

The chief reliance of the Confederate Treasury for
its purchases abroad was at first the specie in the
Southern branch of the United States Mint and
in Southern banks. The former the Confederacy
seized and converted to its own use. Of the latter
it lured into its own hands a very large proportion
by what is commonly called "the fifteen million
loan" — an issue of eight per cent bonds authorized in February, 1861. Most of this specie seems
to have been taken out of the country by the purchase of European commodities. A little, to be
sure, remained, for there was some gold still at
home when the Confederacy fell. But the sum
was small.

In addition to this loan Memminger also per-
suaded Congress on August 19, 1861, to lay a direct
tax — the "war tax," as it was called — of one-
half of one per cent on all property except Confederate bonds and money. As required by the
Constitution this tax was apportioned among the
States, but if it assumed its assessment before
April 1, 1862, each State was to have a reduction
of ten per cent. As there was a general aversion
to the idea of Confederate taxation and a general
faith in loans, what the States did, as a rule, was
to assume their assessment, agree to pay it into

4

the Treasury, and then issue bonds to raise the necessary funds, thus converting the war tax into a loan.

The Confederate, like the Union, Treasury did not have the courage to force the issue upon taxation and leaned throughout the war largely upon loans. It also had recourse to the perilous device of paper money, the gold value of which was not guaranteed. Beginning in March, 1861, it issued under successive laws great quantities of paper notes, some of them interest bearing, some not. It used these notes in payment of its domestic obligations. The purchasing value of the notes soon started on a disastrous downward course, and in 1864 the gold dollar was worth thirty paper dollars. The Confederate Gcvernment thus became involved in a problem of self-preservation that was but half solved by the system of tithes and impressment which we shall encounter later. The depreciation of these notes left governmental clerks without adequate salaries and soldiers without the means of providing for their families. During most of the war, women and other noncombatants had to support the families or else rely upon local charity organized by state or county boards.

Long before all the evils of paper money were experienced, the North, with great swiftness, concentrated its naval forces so as to dominate the Southern ports which had trade relations with Europe. The shipping ports were at once congested with cotton to the great embarrassment of merchants and planters. Partly to relieve them, the Confederate Congress instituted in May, 1861, what is known today as "the hundred million loan." It was the first of a series of "produce loans." The Treasury was authorized to issue eight per cent bonds, to fall due in twenty years, and to sell them for specie or to exchange them for produce or manufactured articles. In the course of the remaining months of 1861 there were exchanged for these bonds great quantities of produce including some 400,000 bales of cotton.

In spite of the distress of the planters, however, the illusion of King Cotton's power does not seem to have been seriously impaired during 1861. In fact, strange as it now seems, the frame of mind of the leaders appears to have been proof, that year, against alarm over the blockade. For two reasons, the Confederacy regarded the blockade at first as a blessing in disguise. It was counted on to act as a protective tariff in stimulating manufactures;

and at the same time the South expected inter-
ruption of the flow of cotton towards Europe
to make England feel her dependence upon the
Confederacy. In this way there would be exerted
an economic coercion which would compel intervention. Such reasoning lay behind a law passed
in May forbidding the export of cotton except
through the seaports of the Confederacy. Similar
laws were enacted by the States. During the
summer, many cotton factors joined in advising
the planters to hold their cotton until the blockade
broke down. In the autumn, the Governor of
Louisiana forbade the export of cotton from New
Orleans. So unshakeable was the illusion in 1861,
that King Cotton had England in his grip! The
illusion died hard. Throughout 1862, and even
in 1863, the newspapers published appeals to the
planters to give up growing cotton for a time, and
even to destroy what they had, so as to coerce the
obdurate. Englishmen.

Meanwhile, Mason had been accorded by the
British upper classes that generous welcome which
they have always extended to the representative of
a people fighting gallantly against odds. During
the hopeful days of 1862 — that Golden Age of
Confederacy — Mason, though not recognized by

the English Government, was shown every kindness by leading members of the aristocracy, who visited him in London and received him at their houses in the country. It was during this period of buoyant hope that the *Alabama* was allowed to go to sea from Liverpool in July, 1862. At the same time Mason heard his hosts express undisguised admiration for the valor of the soldiers serving under Jackson and Lee. Whether he formed any true impression of the other side of British idealism, its resolute opposition to slavery, may be questioned. There seems little doubt that he did not perceive the turning of the tide of English public opinion, in the autumn of 1862, following the Emancipation Proclamation and the great reverses of September and October — Antietam-Sharpsburg, Perryville, Corinth — the backflow of all three of the Confederate offensives.

The cotton famine in England, where perhaps a million people were in actual want through the shutting down of cotton mills, seemed to Mason to be "looming up in fearful proportions." "The public mind," he wrote home in November, 1862, "is very much disturbed by the prospect for the winter; and I am not without hope that it will produce its effects on the councils of the government."

Yet it was the uprising of the British working people in favor of the North that contributed to defeat the one important attempt to intervene in American affairs. Napoleon III had made an offer of mediation which was rejected by the Washington Government early the next year. England and Russia had both declined to participate in Napoleon's scheme, and their refusal marks the beginning of the end of the reign of King Cotton.

At Paris, Slidell was even more hopeful than Mason. He had won over Émile Erlanger, that great banker who was deep in the confidence of Napoleon. So cordial became the relations between the two that it involved their families and led at last to the marriage of Erlanger's son with Slidell's daughter. Whether owing to Slidell's eloquence, or from secret knowledge of the Emperor's designs, or from his own audacity, Erlanger toward the close of 1862 made a proposal that is one of the most daring schemes of financial plunging yet recorded. If the Confederate Government would issue to him bonds secured by cotton, Erlanger would underwrite the bonds, put the proceeds of their sale to the credit of the Confederate agents, and wait for the cotton until it could run the blockade or until peace should be declared. The Confederate Government after some hesitation accepted his plan and issued fifteen millions of "Erlanger bonds," bearing seven per cent, and put them on sale at Paris, London, Amsterdam, and Frankfort.

As a purchaser of these bonds was to be given cotton eventually at a valuation of sixpence a pound, and as cotton was then selling in England for nearly two shillings, the bold gamble caught the fancy of speculators. There was a rush to take up the bonds and to pay the first installment. But before the second installment became due a mysterious change in the market took place and the price of the bonds fell. Holders became alarmed and some even proposed to forfeit their bonds rather than pay on May 1, 1863, the next installment of fifteen per cent of the purchase money. Thereupon Mason undertook to "bull" the market. Agents of the United States Government were supposed to be at the bottom of the drop in the bonds. To defeat their schemes the Confederate agents bought back large amounts in bonds intending to resell. The result was the expenditure of some six million dollars with practically no effect on the market. These "Erlanger bonds" sold slowly through 1863 and even in 1864, and netted a considerable amount to the foreign agents of the Confederacy.

The comparative failure of the Erlanger loan marks the downfall of King Cotton. He was an exploded superstition. He was unable, despite the cotton famine, to coerce the English working-men into siding with a country which they re-garded, because of its support of slavery, as inimi-cal to their interests. At home, the Government confessed the powerlessness of King Cotton by a change of its attitude toward export. During the latter part of the war, the Government secured the meager funds at its disposal abroad by rushing cotton in swift ships through the blockade. So important did this traffic become that the Con-federacy passed stringent laws to keep the control in its own hands. One more cause of friction be-tween the Confederate and the State authorities was thus developed: the Confederate navigation laws prevented the States from running the block-ade on their own account.

The effects of the blockade were felt at the ends of the earth. India became an exporter of cotton. Egypt also entered the competition. That singular dreamer, Ismail Pasha, whose reign made

Egypt briefly an exotic nation, neither eastern nor western, found one of his opportunities in the American War and the failure of the cotton supply.

CHAPTER IV

THE REACTION AGAINST RICHMOND

A POPULAR revulsion of feeling preceded and followed the great period of Confederate history — these six months of Titanic effort which embraced between March and September, 1862, splendid success along with catastrophes. But there was a marked difference between the two tides of popular emotion. The wave of alarm which swept over the South after the surrender of Fort Donelson was quickly translated into such a high passion for battle that the march of events until the day of Antietam resounded like an epic. The failure of the triple offensive which closed this period was followed in very many minds by the appearance of a new temper, often as valiant as the old but far more grim and deeply seamed with distrust. And how is this distrust, of which the Confederate Administration was the object, to be accounted for?

Various answers to this question were made at

the time. The laws of the spring of 1862 were
attacked as unconstitutional. Davis was held
responsible for them and also for the slow equipment of the army. Because the Confederate Congress conducted much of its business in secret
session, the President was charged with a love of
mystery and an unwillingness to take the people
into his confidence. Arrests under the law suspending the writ of *habeas corpus* were made the
texts for harangues on liberty. The right of
freedom of speech was dragged in when General
Van Dorn, in the Southwest, threatened with
suppression any newspaper that published anything which might impair confidence in a commanding officer. How could he have dared to do
this, was the cry, unless the President was behind
him? And when General Bragg assumed a similar
attitude toward the press, the same cry was raised.
Throughout the summer of victories, even while
the thrilling stories of Seven Pines, the Peninsula,
Second Manassas, were sounding like trumpets,
these mutterings of discontent formed an ominous
accompaniment.

Yancey, speaking of the disturbed temper of the
time, attributed it to the general lack of information on the part of Southern people as to what the

Confederate Government was doing. His proposed remedy was an end of the censorship which that Government was attempting to maintain, the abandonment of the secret sessions of its Congress, and the taking of the people into its full confidence. Now a Senator from Alabama, he attempted, at the opening of the congressional session in the autumn of 1862, to abolish secret sessions, but in his efforts he was not successful.

There seems little doubt that the Confederate Government had blundered in being too secretive. Even from Congress, much information was withheld. A curious incident has preserved what appeared to the military mind the justification of this reticence. The Secretary of War refused to comply with a request for information, holding that he could not do so "without disclosing the strength of our armies to many persons of subordinate position whose secrecy cannot be relied upon." "I beg leave to remind you," said he, "of a report made in response to a similar one from the Federal Congress, communicated to them in secret session, and now a part of our archives."

How much the country was in the dark with regard to some vital matters is revealed by an attack on the Confederate Administration which

was made by the Charleston *Mercury*, in February.
The Southern Government was accused of un-
pardonable slowness in sending agents to Europe
to purchase munitions. In point of fact, the Confederate Government had been more prompt than
the Union Government in rushing agents abroad.
But the country was not permitted to know this.
Though the *Courier* was a government organ in
Charleston, it did not meet the charges of the
Mercury by disclosing the facts about the arduous
attempts of the Confederate Government to secure
arms in Europe. The reply of the *Courier* to the
Mercury, though spirited, was all in general terms.
"To shake confidence in Jefferson Davis," said
the *Courier*, "is . . . to bring 'hideous ruin and
combustion' down upon our dearest hopes and
interests." It made "Mr. Davis and his defensive policy" objects of all admiration; called Davis
"our Moses." It was deeply indignant because
it had been "reliably informed that men of high
official position among us" were "calling for a
General Convention of the Confederate States
to depose him and set up a military Dictator in
his place." The *Mercury* retorted that, as to the
plot against "our Moses," there was no evidence
of its existence except the *Courier's* assertion.

Nevertheless, it considered Davis "an incubus to the cause." The controversy between the *Mercury* and the *Courier* at Charleston was paralleled at Richmond by the constant bickering between the government organ, the *Enquirer*, and the *Examiner*, which shares with the *Mercury* the first place among the newspapers hostile to Davis.[1]

Associated with the *Examiner* was a vigorous writer having considerable power of the old-fashioned, furious sort, ever ready to foam at the mouth. If he had had more restraint and less credulity, Edward A. Pollard might have become a master of the art of vituperation. Lacking these qualities, he never rose far above mediocrity. But his fury was so determined and his prejudice so invincible that his writings have something of the power of conviction which fanaticism wields. In midsummer, 1862, Pollard published a book entitled *The First Year of the War*, which was com-

[1] The Confederate Government did not misapprehend the attitude of the intellectual opposition. Its foreign organ, *The Index*, published in London, characterized the leading Southern papers for the enlightenment of the British public. While the *Enquirer* and the *Courier* were singled out as the great champions of the Confederate Government, the *Examiner* and the *Mercury* were portrayed as its arch enemies. The *Examiner* was called the "Ishmael of the Southern press." The *Mercury* was described as "almost rabid on the subject of state rights."

mended by his allies in Charleston as showing no "tendency toward unfairness of statement" and as expressing views "mainly in accordance with popular opinion."

This book, while affecting to be an historical review, was skillfully designed to discredit the Confederate Administration. Almost every disaster, every fault of its management was traceable more or less directly to Davis. Kentucky had been occupied by the Federal army because of the "dull expectation" in which the Confederate Government had stood aside waiting for things somehow to right themselves. The Southern Congress had been criminally slow in coming to conscription, contenting itself with an army of 400,000 men that existed "on paper." "The most distressing abuses were visible in the ill-regulated hygiene of our camps." According to this book, the Confederate Administration was solely to blame for the loss of Roanoke Island. In calling that disaster "deeply humiliating," as he did in a message to Congress, Davis was trying to shield his favorite Benjamin at the cost of gallant soldiers who had been sacrificed through his incapacity. Davis's promotion of Benjamin to the State Department was an act of "ungracious and reckless defiance of popular sentiment." The President was "not the man to consult the sentiment and wisdom of the people; he desired to signalize the infallibility of his own intellect in every measure of the revolution and to identify, from motives of vanity, his own personal genius with every event and detail of the remarkable period of history in which he had been called upon to act. This imperious conceit seemed to swallow up every other idea in his mind." The generals "fretted under this pragmatism" of one whose "vanity" directed the war "from his cushioned seat in Richmond" by means of the one formula, "the defensive policy."

One of Pollard's chief accusations against the Confederate Government was its failure to enforce the conscription law. His paper, the *Examiner*, as well as the *Mercury*, supported Davis in the policy of conscription, but both did their best, first, to rob him of the credit for it and, secondly, to make his conduct of the policy appear inefficient. Pollard claimed for the *Examiner* the credit of having originated the policy of conscription; the *Mercury* claimed it for Rhett.

In other words, an aggressive war party led by the *Examiner* and the *Mercury* had been formed in those early days when the Confederate Government appeared to be standing wholly on the defensive, and when it had failed to confide to the people the extenuating circumstance that lack of arms compelled it to stand still whether it would or no. And yet, after this Government had changed its policy and had taken up in the summer of 1862 an offensive policy, this party — or faction, or what you will — continued its career of opposition. That the secretive habit of the Confederate Government helped cement the opposition cannot be doubted. It is also likely that this opposition gave a vent to certain jealous spirits who had missed the first place in leadership.

Furthermore, the issue of state sovereignty had been raised. In Georgia a movement had begun which was distinctly different from the Virginia-Carolina movement of opposition, a movement for which Rhett and Pollard had scarcely more than disdainful tolerance, and not always that. This parallel opposition found vent, as did the other, in a political pamphlet. On the subject of conscription Davis and the Governor of Georgia — that same Joseph E. Brown who had seized Fort Pulaski in the previous year — exchanged a rancorous correspondence. Their letters were pub-

5

lished in a pamphlet of which Pollard said scorn-
fully that it was hawked about in every city of the
South. Brown, taking alarm at the power given
the Confederate Government by the Conscription
Act, eventually defined his position, and that of
a large following, in the extreme words: "No act
of the Government of the United States prior to
the secession of Georgia struck a blow at constitutional liberty so fell as has been stricken by the
conscript acts."

There were other elements of discontent which
were taking form as early as the autumn of 1862
but which were not yet clearly defined. But the
two obvious sources of internal criticism just
described were enough to disquiet the most resolute
administration. When the triple offensive broke
down, when the ebb-tide began, there was already
everything that was needed to precipitate a political crisis. And now the question arises whether
the Confederate Administration had itself to
blame. Had Davis proved inadequate in his great
undertaking?

The one undeniable mistake of the Government
previous to the autumn of 1862 was its excessive
secrecy. As to the other mistakes attributed to
it at the time, there is good reason to call them

misfortunes. Today we can see that the financial situation, the cotton situation, the relations with Europe, the problem of equipping the armies, were all to a considerable degree beyond the control of the Confederate Government. If there is anything to be added to its mistaken secrecy as a definite cause of irritation, it must be found in the general tone given to its actions by its chief directors. And here there is something to be said.

With all his high qualities of integrity, courage, faithfulness, and zeal, Davis lacked that insight into human life which marks the genius of the supreme executive. He was not an artist in the use of men. He had not that artistic sense of his medium which distinguishes the statesman from the bureaucrat. In fact, he had a dangerous bent toward bureaucracy. As Reuben Davis said of him, "Gifted with some of the highest attributes of a statesman, he lacked the pliancy which enables a man to adapt his measures to the crisis." Furthermore, he lacked humor; there was no safety-valve to his intense nature; and he was a man of delicate health. Mrs. Davis, describing the effects which nervous dyspepsia and neuralgia had upon him, says he would come home from his office "fasting, a mere mass of throbbing nerves, and perfectly exhausted." And it cannot be denied that his mind was dogmatic. Here are dangerous lines for the character of a leader of revolution — the bureaucratic tendency, something of rigidity, lack of humor, physical wretchedness, dogmatism. Taken together, they go far toward explaining his failure in judging men, his irritable confidence in himself.

It is no slight detail of a man's career to be placed side by side with a genius of the first rank without knowing it. But Davis does not seem ever to have appreciated that the man commanding in the Seven Days' Battles was one of the world's supreme characters. The relation between Davis and Lee was always cordial, and it brought out Davis's character in its best light. Nevertheless, so rooted was Davis's faith in his own abilities that he was capable of saying, at a moment of acutest anxiety, "If I could take one wing and Lee the other, I think we could between us wrest a victory from those people." And yet, his military experience embraced only the minor actions of a young officer on the Indian frontier and the gallant conduct of a subordinate in the Mexican War. He had never executed a great military design. His desire for the military life was, after all, his only ground for ranking himself with the victor of Second Manassas. Davis was also unfortunate in lacking the power to overcome men and sweep them along with him — the power Lee showed so conspicuously. Nor was Davis averse to sharp reproof of the highest officials when he thought them in the wrong. He once wrote to Joseph E. Johnston that a letter of his contained "arguments and statements utterly unfounded" and "insinuations as unfounded as they were unbecoming."

Davis was not always wise in his choice of men. His confidence in Bragg, who was long his chief military adviser, is not sustained by the military critics of a later age. His Cabinet, though not the contemptible body caricatured by the malice of Pollard, was not equal to the occasion. Of the three men who held the office of Secretary of State, Toombs and Hunter had little if any qualification for such a post, while the third, Benjamin, is the sphinx of Confederate history.

In a way, Judah P. Benjamin is one of the most interesting men in American politics. By descent a Jew, born in the West Indies, he spent his boyhood mainly at Charleston and his college days at Yale. He went to New Orleans to begin his illustrious career as a lawyer, and from Louisiana entered politics. The facile keenness of his intellect is beyond dispute. He had the Jewish clarity of thought, the wonderful Jewish detachment in matters of pure mind. But he was also an American of the middle of the century. His quick and responsive nature — a nature that enemies might call simulative — caught and reflected the characteristics of that singular and highly rhetorical age. He lives in tradition as the man of the constant smile, and yet there is no one in history whose state papers contain passages of fiercer violence in days of tension. How much of his violence was genuine, how much was a manner of speaking, his biographers have not had the courage to determine. Like so many American biographers they have avoided the awkward questions and have glanced over, as lightly as possible, the persistent attempts of Congress to drive him from office.

Nothing could shake the resolution of Davis to retain Benjamin in the Cabinet. Among Davis's loftiest qualities was his sense of personal loyalty. Once he had given his confidence, no amount of opposition could shake his will but served rather to harden him. When Benjamin as Secretary of War passed under a cloud, Davis led him forth resplendent as Secretary of State. Whether he was wise in doing so, whether the opposition was not justified in its distrust of Benjamin, is still an open question. What is certain is that both these able men, even before the crisis that arose in the autumn of 1862, had rendered themselves and their Government widely unpopular. It must never be forgotten that Davis entered office without the backing of any definite faction. He was a "dark horse," a compromise candidate. To build up a stanch following, to create enthusiasm for his Administration, was a prime necessity of his first year as President. Yet he seems not to have realized this necessity. Boldly, firmly, dogmatically, he gave his whole thought and his entire energy to organizing the Government in such a way that it could do its work efficiently. And therein may have been the proverbial rift within the lute. To Davis statecraft was too much a thing of methods and measures, too little a thing of men and passions.

During the autumn of 1862 and the following winter the disputes over the conduct of the war began to subside and two other themes became prominent: the sovereignty of the States, which appeared to be menaced by the Government, and

the personality of Davis, whom malcontents regarded as a possible despot. Contrary to tradition,
the first note of alarm over state rights was not
struck by its great apostle Rhett, although the
note was sounded in South Carolina in the early
autumn. There existed in this State at that time
an extra assembly called the "Convention," which
had been organized in 1860 for the general purpose
of seeing the State through the "revolution." In
the Convention, in September, 1862, the question
of a contest with the Confederate Government on
the subject of a state army was definitely raised.
It was proposed to organize a state army and to
instruct the Legislature to "take effectual measures
to prevent the agents of the Confederate Government from raising troops in South Carolina except
by voluntary enlistment or by applying to the
Executive of the State to call out the militia as by
law organized, or some part of it to be mustered
into the Confederate service." This proposal
brought about a sharp debate upon the Confederate Government and its military policy. Rhett
made a remarkable address, which should of itself
quiet forever the old tale that he was animated
in his opposition solely by the pique of a disappointed candidate for the presidency. Though

as sharp as ever against the Government and though agreeing wholly with the spirit of the state army plan, he took the ground that circumstances at the moment rendered the organization of such an army inopportune. A year earlier he would have strongly supported the plan. In fact, in opposition to Davis he had at that time, he said, urged an obligatory army which the States should be required to raise. The Confederate Administration, however, had defeated his scheme. Since then the situation had changed and had become so serious that now there was no choice but to submit to military necessity. He regarded the general conscription law as "absolutely necessary to save" the Confederacy "from utter devastation if not final subjugation. Right or wrong, the policy of the Administration had left us no other alternative. . . ."

The dominant attitude in South Carolina in the autumn of 1862 is in strong contrast, because of its firm grasp upon fact, with the attitude of the Brown faction in Georgia. An extended history of the Confederate movement — one of those vast histories that delight the recluse and scare away the man of the world — would labor to build up images of what might be called the personalities of the four States that continued from the beginning to the end parts of the effective Confederate system — Virginia, the two Carolinas, and Georgia. We are prone to forget that the Confederacy was practically divided into separate units as early as the capture of New Orleans by Farragut, but a great history of the time would have a special and thrilling story of the conduct of the detached western unit, the isolated world of Louisiana, Arkansas, and Texas — the "Department of the Trans-Mississippi" — cut off from the main body of the Confederacy and hemmed in between the Federal army and the deep sea. Another group of States — Tennessee, Mississippi, Alabama — became so soon, and remained so long, a debatable land, on which the two armies fought, that they also had scant opportunity for genuine political life. Florida, small and exposed, was absorbed in its gallant achievement of furnishing to the armies a number of soldiers larger than its voting population.

Thus, after the loss of New Orleans, one thing with another operated to confine the area of full political life to Virginia and her three neighbors to the South. And yet even among these States there was no political solidarity or unanimity of opinion, for the differences in their past experience, social structure, and economic conditions made for distinct points of view. In South Carolina, particularly, the prevailing view was that of experienced, disillusioned men who realized from the start that secession had burnt their bridges, and that now they must win the fight or change the whole current of their lives. In the midst of the extraordinary conditions of war, they never talked as if their problems were the problems of peace. Brown, on the other hand, had but one way of reasoning — if we are to call it reasoning — and, with Hannibal at the gates, talked as if the control of the situation were still in his own hands.

While South Carolina, so grimly conscious of the reality of war and the danger of internal discord, held off from the issue of state sovereignty, the Brown faction in Georgia blithely pressed it home. A bill for extending the conscription age which was heartily advocated by the *Mercury* was as heartily condemned by Brown. To the President he wrote announcing his continued opposition to a law which he declared "encroaches upon the reserved rights of the State and strikes down her sovereignty at a single blow." Though the Supreme Court of Georgia pronounced the conscription acts constitutional, the Governor and his faction did not cease to condemn them.   Linton Stephens, as well as his famous kinsman, took up the cudgels.   In a speech before the Georgia Legislature, in November, Linton Stephens borrowed almost exactly the Governor's phraseology in denying the necessity for conscription, and this continued to be the note of their faction throughout the war.   "Conscription checks enthusiasm," was ever their cry; "we are invincible under a system of volunteering, we are lost with conscription."

Meanwhile the military authorities looked facts in the face and had a different tale to tell.   They complained that in various parts of the country, especially in the mountain districts, they were unable to obtain men.   Lee reported that his army melted away before his eye and asked for an increase of authority to compel stragglers to return.   At the same time Brown was quarreling with the Administration as to who should name the officers of the Georgia troops.   Zebulon B. Vance, the newly elected Governor of North Carolina and an anti-Davis man, said to the Legislature: "It is mortifying to find entire brigades of North Carolina soldiers commanded by strangers, and in many cases our own brave and war-worn colonels are made to give place to colonels from distant States." In addition to such indications of discontent a vast mass of evidence makes plain the opposition to conscription toward the close of 1862 and the looseness of various parts of the military system.

It was a moment of intense excitement and of nervous strain. The country was unhappy, for it had lost faith in the Government at Richmond. The blockade was producing its effect. European intervention was receding into the distance. One of the characteristics of the editorials and speeches of this period is a rising tide of bitterness against England. Napoleon's proposal in November to mediate, though it came to naught, somewhat revived the hope of an eventual recognition of the Confederacy but did not restore buoyancy to the people of the South. The Emancipation Proclamation, though scoffed at as a cry of impotence, none the less increased the general sense of crisis.

Worst of all, because of its immediate effect upon the temper of the time, food was very scarce and prices had risen to indefensible heights. The army was short of shoes. In the newspapers, as winter came on, were to be found touching descriptions of Lee's soldiers standing barefoot in the snow. A flippant comment of Benjamin's, that the shoes had probably been traded for whiskey, did not tend to improve matters. Even though short of supplies themselves, the people as a whole eagerly subscribed to buy shoes for the army.

There was widespread and heartless speculation in the supplies. Months previous the *Courier* had made this ominous editorial remark: "Speculators and monopolists seem determined to force the people everywhere to the full exercise of all the remedies allowed by law." In August, 1862, the Governor of Florida wrote to the Florida delegation at Richmond urging them to take steps to meet the "nefarious smuggling" of speculators who charged extortionate prices. In September, he wrote again begging for legislation to compel millers, tanners, and saltmakers to offer their products at reasonable rates. As these men were exempt from military duty because their labor was held to be a public service, feeling against them ran high. Governor Vance proposed a state convention to regulate prices for North Carolina and by proclamation forbade the export of provisions in order to prevent the seeking of exorbitant prices in other markets. Davis wrote to various Governors urging them to obtain state legislation

JOHN C. BRECKINRIDGE

Photograph by Brady.

JOHN C. BRECKINRIDGE.

Photograph by Brady.

to reduce extortion in the food business. In the provisioning of the army the Confederate Government had recourse to impressment and the arbitrary fixing of prices. Though the Attorney-General held this action to be constitutional, it led to sharp contentions; and at length a Virginia court granted an injunction to a speculator who had been paid by the Government for flour less than it had cost him.

In an attempt to straighten out this tangled situation, the Confederate Government began, late in 1862, by appointing as its new Secretary of War,[1] James A. Seddon of Virginia — at that time high in popular favor. The *Mercury* hailed his advent with transparent relief, for no appointment could have seemed to it more promising. Indeed, as the new year (1863) opened the *Mercury* was in better humor with the Administration than perhaps at any other time during the war. To the President's message it gave praise that was almost cordial. This amicable temper was short-lived, however, and three months later the heavens had clouded

[1] There were in all six Secretaries of War: Leroy P. Walker, until September 16, 1861; Judah P. Benjamin, until March 18, 1862; George W. Randolph, until November 17, 1862; Gustavus W. Smith (temporarily), until November 21, 1862; James A. Seddon, until February 6, 1865; General John C. Breckinridge.

again, for the Government had entered upon a course that consolidated the opposition in anger and distrust.

Early in 1863 the Confederate Government presented to the country a program in which the main features were three. Of these the two which did not rouse immediate hostility in the party of the *Examiner* and the *Mercury* were the Impressment Act of March, 1863 (amended by successive acts), and the act known as the Tax in Kind, which was approved the following month. Though the Impressment Act subsequently made vast trouble for the Government, at the time of its passage its beneficial effects were not denied. To it was attributed by the Richmond *Whig* the rapid fall of prices in April, 1863. Corn went down at Richmond from $12 and $10 a bushel to $4.20, and flour dropped in North Carolina from $45 a barrel to $25. Under this act commissioners were appointed in each State jointly by the Confederate President and the Governor with the duty of fixing prices for government transactions and of publishing every two months an official schedule of the prices to be paid by the Government for the supplies which it impressed.

The new Tax Act attempted to provide revenues

which should not be paid in depreciated currency.
With no bullion to speak of, the Confederate Congress could not establish a circulating medium with
even an approximation to constant value. Realiz-
ing this situation, Memminger had advised falling
back on the ancient system of tithes and the support of the Government by direct contributions
of produce. After licensing a great number of
occupations and laying a property tax and an
income tax, the new law demanded a tenth of the
produce of all farmers. On this law the *Mercury*
pronounced a benediction in an editorial on *The
Fall of Prices*, which it attributed to "the healthy
influence of the tax bill which has just become
law."[1]

Had these two measures been the whole program of the Government, the congressional session
of the spring of 1863 would have had a different
significance in Confederate history. But there was
a third measure that provoked a new attack on the
Government. The gracious words of the *Mercury*
on the tax in kind came as an interlude in the

[1] The fall of prices was attributed by others to a funding act, — one
of several passed by the Confederate Congress — which, in March,
1863, aimed by various devices to contract the volume of the currency.
It was very generally condemned, and it anticipated the yet more drastic measure, the Funding Act of 1864, which will be described later.

6

midst of a bitter controversy. An editorial of the 12th of March headed *A Despotism over the Confederate States Proposed in Congress* amounted to a declaration of war. From this time forward the opposition and the Government drew steadily further and further apart and their antagonism grew steadily more relentless.

What caused this irrevocable breach was a bill introduced into the House by Ethelbert Barksdale of Mississippi, an old friend of President Davis. This bill would have invested the President with authority to suspend the privilege of the writ of *habeas corpus* in any part of the Confederacy, whenever in his judgment such suspension was desirable. The first act suspending the privilege of *habeas corpus* had long since expired and applied only to such regions as were threatened with invasion. It had served usefully under martial law in cleansing Richmond of its rogues, and also had been in force at Charleston. The *Mercury* had approved it and had exhorted its readers to take the matter sensibly as an inevitable detail of war. Between that act and the act now proposed the *Mercury* saw no similarity. Upon the merits of the question it fought a furious journalistic duel with the *Enquirer*, the government organ at Richmond, which insisted that President Davis would not abuse his power. The *Mercury* replied that if he "were a second Washington, or an angel upon earth, the degradation such a surrender of our rights implies would still be abhorrent to every freeman." In retort the *Enquirer* pointed out that a similar law had been enacted by another Congress with no bad results. And in point of fact the *Enquirer* was right, for in October, 1862, after the expiration of the first act suspending the privilege of the writ of *habeas corpus*, Congress passed a second giving to the President the immense power which was now claimed for him again. This second act was in force several months. Then the *Mercury* made the astounding declaration that it had never heard of the second act, and thereupon proceeded to attack the secrecy of the Administration with renewed vigor.

On this issue of reviving the expired second *Habeas Corpus* Act, a battle royal was fought in the Confederate Congress. The forces of the Administration defended the new measure on the ground that various regions were openly seditious and that conscription could not be enforced without it. This argument gave a new text for the cry of "despotism." The congressional leader of the opposition was Henry S. Foote, once the rival of Davis in Mississippi and now a citizen of Tennessee. Fierce, vindictive, sometimes convincing, always shrewd, he was a powerful leader of the rough and ready, buccaneering sort.   Under his guidance the debate was diverted into a rancorous discussion of the conduct of the generals in the execution of martial law.   Foote pulled out all the stops in the organ of political rhetoric and went in for a chant royal of righteous indignation.   The main object of this attack was General Hindman and his doings in Arkansas.   Those were still the days of pamphleteering.   Though General Albert Pike had written a severe pamphlet condemning Hindman, to this pamphlet the Confederate Government had shut its eyes.   Foote, however, flourished it in the face of the House.   He thundered forth his belief that Hindman was worse even than the man most detested in the South, than "beast Butler himself, for the latter is only charged with persecuting and oppressing the avowed enemies of his Government, while Hindman, if guilty as charged, has practised cruelties unnumbered" on his people.   Other representatives spoke in the same vein.   Baldwin of Virginia told harrowing tales of martial law in that State.   Barksdale attempted to retaliate, sarcastically reminding him of a recent scene of riot and disorder which proved that martial law, in any effective form, did not exist in Virginia. He alluded to a riot, ostensibly for bread, in which an Amazonian woman had led a mob to the pillaging of the Richmond jewelry shops, a riot which Davis himself had quelled by meeting the rioters and threatening to fire upon them. But sarcasm proved powerless against Foote. His climax was a lurid tale of a soldier who while marching past his own house heard that his wife was dying, who left the ranks for a last word with her, and who on rejoining the command, "hoping to get permission to bury her," was shot as a deserter. And there was no one on the Government benches to anticipate Kipling and cry out "flat art!" Resolutions condemning martial law were passed by a vote of 45 to 27.

Two weeks later the *Mercury* preached a burial sermon over the Barksdale Bill, which had now been rejected by the House. Congress was about to adjourn, and before it reassembled elections for the next House would be held. "The measure is dead for the present," said the *Mercury*, "but power is ever restive and prone to accumulate power; and if the war continues, other efforts will doubtless be made to make the President a Dictator. Let the people keep their eyes steadily fixed on their representatives with respect to this vital matter; and should the effort again be made to suspend the Habeas Corpus Act, demand that a recorded vote should show those who shall strike down their liberties."

CHAPTER V

THE CRITICAL YEAR

THE great military events of the year 1863 have pushed out of men's memories the less dramatic but scarcely less important civil events. To begin with, in this year two of the greatest personalities in the South passed from the political stage: in the summer Yancey died; and in the autumn, Rhett went into retirement.

The ever malicious Pollard insists that Yancey's death was due ultimately to a personal encounter with a Senator from Georgia on the floor of the Senate. The curious may find the discreditable story embalmed in the secret journal of the Senate, where are the various motions designed to keep the incident from the knowledge of the world. Whether it really caused Yancey's death is another question. However, the moment of his passing has dramatic significance. Just as the battle over conscription was fully begun, when the fear that the

Confederate Government had arrayed itself against the rights of the States had definitely taken shape, when this dread had been reënforced by the alarm over the suspension of *habeas corpus*, the great pioneer of the secession movement went to his grave, despairing of the country he had failed to lead. His death occurred in the same month as the Battle of Gettysburg, at the very time when the Confederacy was dividing against itself.

The withdrawal of Rhett from active life was an incident of the congressional elections. He had consented to stand for Congress in the Third District of South Carolina but was defeated. The full explanation of the vote is still to be made plain; it seems clear, however, that South Carolina at this time knew its own mind quite positively. Five of the six representatives returned to the Second Congress, including Rhett's opponent, Lewis M. Ayer, had sat in the First Congress. The subsequent history of the South Carolina delegation and of the State Government shows that by 1863 South Carolina had become, broadly speaking, on almost all issues an anti-Davis State. And yet the largest personality and probably the ablest mind in the State was rejected as a candidate for Congress. No character in American history is a finer challenge to the biographer than this powerful figure of Rhett, who in 1861 at the supreme crisis of his life seemed the master of his world and yet in every lesser crisis was a comparative failure. As in Yancey, so in Rhett, there was something that fitted him to one great moment but did not fit him to others. There can be little doubt that his defeat at the polls of his own district deeply mortified him. He withdrew from politics, and though he doubtless, through the editorship of one of his sons, inspired the continued opposition of the *Mercury* to the Government, Rhett himself hardly reappears in Confederate history except for a single occasion during the debate a year later upon the burning question of arming the slaves.

The year was marked by very bitter attacks upon President Davis on the part of the opposition press. The *Mercury* revived the issue of the conduct of the war which had for some time been overshadowed by other issues. In the spring, to be sure, things had begun to look brighter, and Chancellorsville had raised Lee's reputation to its zenith. The disasters of the summer, Gettysburg and Vicksburg, were for a time minimized by the Government and do not appear to have caused the alarm which their strategic importance might well have created. But when in the latter days of July the facts became generally known, the *Mercury* arraigned the President's conduct of the war as "a vast complication of incompetence and folly"; it condemned the whole scheme of the Northern invasion and maintained that Lee should have stood on the defensive while twenty or thirty thousand men were sent to the relief of Vicksburg. These two ideas it bitterly reiterated and in August went so far as to quote Macaulay's famous passage on Parliament's dread of a decisive victory over Charles and to apply it to Davis in unrestrained language that reminds one of Pollard.

Equally unrestrained were the attacks upon other items of the policy of the Confederate Government. The Impressment Law began to be a target. Farmers who were compelled to accept the prices fixed by the impressment commissioners cried out that they were being ruined. Men of the stamp of Toombs came to their assistance with railing accusations such as this: "I have heard it said that we should not sacrifice liberty to independence, but I tell you, my countrymen, that the two are inseparable. . . . If we lose our liberty we shall lose our independence. . . . I would rather see the whole country the cemetery of freedom than the habitation of slaves." Protests which poured in upon the Government insisted that the power to impress supplies did not carry with it the power to fix prices. Worthy men, ridden by the traditional ideas of political science and unable to modify these in the light of the present emergency, wailed out their despair over the "usurpation" of Richmond.

The tax in kind was denounced in the same vein. The licensing provisions of this law and its income tax did not satisfy the popular imagination. These provisions concerned the classes that could borrow. The classes that could not borrow, that had no resources but their crops, felt that they were being driven to the wall. The bitter saying went around that it was "a rich man's war and a poor man's fight." As land and slaves were not directly taxed, the popular discontent appeared to have ground for its anger. Furthermore, it must never be forgotten that this was the first general tax that the poor people of the South were ever conscious of paying. To people who knew the tax-gatherer as little more than a mythical being, he suddenly appeared like a malevolent creature who swept off ruthlessly the tenth of their produce. It is not strange that an intemperate reaction against the planters and their leadership followed. The illusion spread that they were not doing their share of the fighting; and as rich men were permitted to hire substitutes to represent them in the army, this really baseless report was easily propped up in the public mind with what appeared to be reason.

In North Carolina, where the peasant farmer was a larger political factor than in any other State, this feeling against the Confederate Government because of the tax in kind was most dangerous. In the course of the summer, while the military fortunes of the Confederacy were toppling at Vicksburg and Gettysburg, the North Carolina farmers in a panic of self-preservation held numerous meetings of protest and denunciation. They expressed their thoughtless terror in resolutions asserting that the action of Congress "in secret session, without consulting with their constituents at home, taking from the hard laborers of the Confederacy one-tenth of the people's living, instead of taking back their own currency in tax, is unjust and tyrannical." Other resolutions called the tax "unconstitutional, anti-republican, and oppressive"; and still others pledged the farmers "to resist to the bitter end any such monarchical tax."

A leader of the discontented in North Carolina was found in W. W. Holden, the editor of the *Raleigh Progress*, who before the war had attempted to be spokesman for the men of small property by advocating taxes on slaves and similar measures. He proposed as the conclusion of the whole matter the opening of negotiations for peace. We shall see later how deep-seated was this singular delusion that peace could be had for the asking. In 1863, however, many men in North Carolina took up the suggestion with delight. Jonathan Worth wrote in his diary, on hearing that the influential *North Carolina Standard* had come out for peace: "I still abhor, as I always did, this accursed war and the wicked men, North and South, who inaugurated it. The whole country at the North and the South is a great military despotism." With such discontent in the air, the elections in North Carolina drew near. The feeling was intense and riots occurred. Newspaper offices were demolished — among them Holden's, to destroy which a detachment of passing soldiers converted itself into a mob. In the western counties deserters from the army, combined in bands, were joined by other deserters from Tennessee, and terrorized the countryside. Governor Vance, alarmed at the progress which this disorder was making, issued a proclamation imploring his rebellious countrymen to conduct in a peaceable manner their campaign for the repeal of obnoxious laws.

The measure of political unrest in North Carolina was indicated in the autumn when a new delegation to Congress was chosen. Of the ten who composed it, eight were new men. Though they did not stand for a clearly defined program, they represented on the whole anti-Davis tendencies. The Confederate Administration had failed to carry the day in the North Carolina elections; and in Georgia there were even more sweeping evidences of unrest. Of the ten representatives chosen for the Second Congress nine had not sat in the First, and Georgia now was in the main frankly anti-Davis. There had been set up at Richmond a new organ of the Government called the *Sentinel*, which was more entirely under the presidential shadow than even the *Enquirer* and the *Courier*. Speaking of the elections, the *Sentinel* deplored the "upheaval of political elements" revealed by the defeat of so many tried representatives whose constituents had not returned them to the Second Congress.

What was Davis doing while the ground was

thus being cut from under his feet? For one thing he gave his endorsement to the formation of "Confederate Societies" whose members bound themselves to take Confederate money as legal tender. He wrote a letter to one such society in Mississippi, praising it for attempting "by common consent to bring down the prices of all articles to the standard of the soldiers' wages" and adding that the passion of speculation had "seduced citizens of all classes from a determined prosecution of the war to an effort to amass money." The *Sentinel* advocated the establishment of a law fixing maximum prices. The discussion of this proposal seems to make plain the *raison d'être* for the existence of the *Sentinel*. Even such stanch government organs as the *Enquirer* and the *Courier* shied at the idea, but the *Mercury* denounced it vigorously, giving long extracts from Thiers, and discussed the mistakes of the French Revolution with its "law of maximum."

Davis, however, did not take an active part in the political campaign, nor did the other members of the Government. It was not because of any notion that the President should not leave the capital that Davis did not visit the disaffected regions of North Carolina when the startled populace winced under its first experience with taxation. Three times during his Administration Davis left Richmond on extended journeys: late in 1862, when Vicksburg had become a chief concern of the Government, he went as far afield as Mississippi in order to get entirely in touch with the military situation in those parts; in the month of October, 1863, when there was another moment of intense military anxiety, Davis again visited the front; and of a third journey which he undertook in 1864, we shall hear in time. It is to be noted that each of these journeys was prompted by a military motive; and here, possibly, we get an explanation of his inadequacy as a statesman. He could not lay aside his interest in military affairs for the supremely important concerns of civil office; and he failed to understand how to ingratiate his Administration by personal appeals to popular imagination.

In October, 1863, — the very month in which his old rival Rhett suffered his final defeat, — Davis undertook a journey because Bragg, after his great victory at Chickamauga, appeared to be letting slip a golden opportunity, and because there were reports of dissension among Bragg's officers and of general confusion in his army. After he had, as he thought, restored harmony in the camp, Davis turned southward on a tour of appeal and inspiration. He went as far as Mobile, and returning bent his course through Charleston, where, at the beginning of November, less than two weeks after Rhett's defeat, Davis was received with all due formalities. Members of the Rhett family were among those who formally received the President at the railway station. There was a parade of welcome, an official reception, a speech by the President from the steps of the city hall, and much applause by friends of the Administration. But certain ominous signs were not lacking. The *Mercury*, for example, tucked away in an obscure column its account of the event, while its rival, the *Courier*, made the President's visit the feature of the day.

Davis returned to Richmond, early in November, to throw himself again with his whole soul into problems that were chiefly military. He did not realize that the crisis had come and gone and that he had failed to grasp the significance of the internal political situation. The Government had failed to carry the elections and to secure a working majority in Congress. Never again was it to have behind it a firm and confident support. The

7

unity of the secession movement had passed away. Thereafter the Government was always to be regarded with suspicion by the extreme believers in state sovereignty and by those who were sullenly convinced that the burdens of the war were unfairly distributed. And there were not wanting men who were ready to construe each emergency measure as a step toward a *coup d'état.*

CHAPTER VI

LIFE IN THE CONFEDERACY

WHEN the fortunes of the Confederacy in both camp and council began to ebb, the life of the Southern people had already profoundly changed. The gallant, delightful, care-free life of the planter class had been undermined by a war which was eating away its foundations. Economic no less than political forces were taking from the planter that ideal of individual liberty as dear to his heart as it had been, ages before, to his feudal prototype. One of the most important details of the changing situation had been the relation of the Government to slavery. The history of the Confederacy had opened with a clash between the extreme advocates of slavery — the slavery-at-any-price men — and the Administration. The Confederate Congress had passed a bill ostensibly to make effective the clause in its constitution prohibiting the African slave-trade. The quick eye of Davis had detected in it a mode of evasion, for cargoes of captured slaves were to be confiscated and sold at public auction. The President had exposed this adroit subterfuge in his message vetoing the bill, and the slavery-at-any-price men had not sufficient influence in Congress to override the veto, though they muttered against it in the public press.

The slavery-at-any-price men did not again conspicuously show their hands until three years later when the Administration included emancipation in its policy.   The ultimate policy of emancipation was forced upon the Government by many considerations but more particularly by the difficulty of securing labor for military purposes.   In a country where the supply of fighting men was limited and the workers were a class apart, the Government had to employ the only available laborers or confess its inability to meet the industrial demands of war.   But the available laborers were slaves.   How could their services be secured? By purchase?   Or by conscription?   Or by temporary impressment?

Though Davis and his advisers were prepared to face all the hazards involved in the purchase or confiscation of slaves, the traditional Southern temper instantly recoiled from the suggestion.   A

Government possessed of great numbers of slaves, whether bought or appropriated, would have in its hands a gigantic power, perhaps for industrial competition with private owners, perhaps even for organized military control. Besides, the Government might at any moment by emancipating its slaves upset the labor system of the country. Furthermore, the opportunities for favoritism in the management of state-owned slaves were beyond calculation. Considerations such as these therefore explain the watchful jealousy of the planters toward the Government whenever it proposed to acquire property in slaves.

It is essential not to attribute this social-political dread of government ownership of slaves merely to the clutch of a wealthy class on its property. Too many observers, strangely enough, see the latter motive to the exclusion of the former. Davis himself was not, it would seem, free from this confusion. He insisted that neither slaves nor land were taxed by the Confederacy, and between the lines he seems to attribute to the planter class the familiar selfishness of massed capital. He forgot that the tax in kind was combined with an income tax. In theory, at least, the slave and the land — even non-farming land — were taxed. However, the dread of a slave-owning Government prevented any effective plan for supplying the army with labor except through the temporary impressment of slaves who were eventually to be returned to their owners. The policy of emancipation had to wait.

Bound up in the labor question was the question of the control of slaves during the war. In the old days when there were plenty of white men in the countryside, the roads were carefully patrolled at night, and no slave ventured to go at large unless fully prepared to prove his identity. But with the coming of war the comparative smallness of the fighting population made it likely from the first that the countryside everywhere would be stripped of its white guardians. In that event, who would be left to control the slaves? Early in the war a slave police was provided for by exempting from military duty overseers in the ratio approximately of one white to twenty slaves. But the marvelous faithfulness of the slaves, who nowhere attempted to revolt, made these precautions unnecessary. Later laws exempted one overseer on every plantation of fifteen slaves, not so much to perform patrol duty as to increase the productivity of plantation labor.

This "Fifteen Slave" Law was one of many instances that were caught up by the men of small property as evidence that the Government favored the rich. A much less defensible law, and one which was bitterly attacked for the same reason, was the unfortunate measure permitting the hiring of substitutes by men drafted into the army. Eventually, the clamor against this law caused its repeal, but before that time it had worked untold harm as apparent evidence of "a rich man's war and a poor man's fight." Extravagant stories of the avoidance of military duty by the ruling class, though in the main they were mere fairy tales, changed the whole atmosphere of Southern life. The old glad confidence uniting the planter class with the bulk of the people had been impaired. Misapprehension appeared on both sides. Too much has been said lately, however, in justification of the poorer classes who were thus wakened suddenly to a distrust of the aristocracy; and too little has been said of the proud recoil of the aristocracy in the face of a sudden, credulous perversion of its motives — a perversion inspired by the pinching of the shoe, and yet a shoe that pinched one class as hard as it did another. It is as unfair to charge the planter with selfishness in opposing the appropriation of slaves as it is to make the same charge against the small farmers for resisting tithes. In face of the record, the planter comes off somewhat the better of the two; but it must be remembered that he had the better education, the larger mental horizon.

The Confederacy had long recognized women of all classes as the most dauntless defenders of the cause. The women of the upper classes passed without a tremor from a life of smiling ease to a life of extreme hardship. One day, their horizon was without a cloud; another day, their husbands and fathers had gone to the front. Their luxuries had disappeared, and they were reduced to plain hard living, toiling in a thousand ways to find provision and clothing, not only for their own children but for the poorer families of soldiers. The women of the poor throughout the South deserve similar honor. Though the physical shock of the change may not have been so great, they had to face the same deep realities — hunger and want, anxiety over the absent soldiers, solicitude for children, grief for the dead. One of the pathetic aspects of Confederate life was the household composed of several families, all women and children, huddled together without a man or even a half-grown lad to be their link with the mill and the market. In those regions where there were few slaves and the exemption of overseers did not operate, such households were numerous.

The great privations which people endured during the Confederacy have passed into familiar tradition. They are to be traced mainly to three causes: to the blockade, to the inadequate system of transportation, and to the heartlessness of speculators. The blockade was the real destroyer of the South. Besides ruining the whole policy based on King Cotton, besides impeding to a vast extent the inflow of munitions from Europe, it also deprived Southern life of numerous articles which were hard to relinquish — not only such luxuries as tea and coffee, but also such utter necessities as medicines. And though the native herbs were diligently studied, though the Government established medical laboratories with results that were not inconsiderable, the shortage of medicines remained throughout the war a distressing feature of Southern life. The Tredegar Iron Works at Richmond and a foundry at Selma, Alabama, were the only mills in the South capable of casting the heavy ordnance necessary for military purposes. And the demand for powder mills and gun factories to provide for the needs of the army was scarcely greater than the demand for cotton mills and commercial foundries to supply the wants of the civil population.   The Government worked without ceasing to keep pace with the requirements of the situation, and, in view of the immense difficulties which it had to face, it was fairly successful in supplying the needs of the army.   Powder was provided by the Niter and Mining Bureau; lead for Confederate bullets was collected from many sources — even from the window-weights of the houses; iron was brought from the mines of Alabama; guns came from newly built factories; and machines and tools were part of the precious freight of the blockade-runners.   Though the poorly equipped mills turned a portion of the cotton crop into textiles, and though everything that was possible was done to meet the needs of the people, the supply of manufactures was sadly inadequate.   The universal shortage was betrayed by the limitation of the size of most newspapers to a single sheet, and the desperate situation clearly and completely revealed by the way in which, as a last resort, the Confederates were compelled to repair their railroads by pulling up the rails of one road in order to repair another that the necessities of war rendered indispensable.

The railway system, if such it can be called, was one of the weaknesses of the Confederacy. Before the war the South had not felt the need of elaborate interior communication, for its commerce in the main went seaward, and thence to New England or to Europe. Hitherto the railway lines had seen no reason for merging their local character in extensive combinations. Owners of short lines were inclined by tradition to resist even the imperative necessities of war and their stubborn conservatism was frequently encouraged by the short-sighted parochialism of the towns. The same pitiful narrowness that led the peasant farmer to threaten rebellion against the tax in kind led his counterpart in the towns to oppose the War Department in its efforts to establish through railroad lines because they threatened to impair local business interests. A striking instance of this disinclination towards coöperation is the action of Petersburg. Two railroads terminated at this point but did not connect, and it was an ardent desire of the military authorities to link the two and convert them into one. The town, however, unable to see beyond its boundaries and resolute in its determination to save its transfer business, successfully obstructed the needs of the army.[1]

As a result of this lack of efficient organization an immense congestion resulted all along the railroads. Whether this, rather than a failure in supply, explains the approach of famine in the latter part of the war, it is today very difficult to determine. In numerous state papers of the time, the assertion was reiterated that the yield of food was abundant and that the scarcity of food at many places, including the cities and the battle fronts, was due to defects in transportation. Certain it is that the progress of supplies from one point to another was intolerably slow.

All this want of coördination facilitated speculation. We shall see hereafter how merciless this speculation became and we shall even hear of profits on food rising to more than four hundred per cent. However, the oft-quoted prices of the later years — when, for instance, a pair of shoes cost a hundred dollars — signify little, for they rested on an inflated currency. None the less they inspired the witticism that one should take money to market in a basket and bring provisions home

---

[1] See an article on *The Confederate Government and the Railroads* in the *American Historical Review*, July, 1917, by Charles W. Ramsdell.

in one's pocketbook. Endless stories could be told of speculators hoarding food and watching unmoved the sufferings of a famished people. Said Bishop Pierce, in a sermon before the General Assembly of Georgia, on Fast Day, in March, 1863: "Restlessness and discontent prevail. . . . Extortion, pitiless extortion is making havoc in the land. We are devouring each other. Avarice with full barns puts the bounties of Providence under bolts and bars, waiting with eager longings for higher prices. . . . The greed of gain . . . stalks among us unabashed by the heroic sacrifice of our women or the gallant deeds of our soldiers. Speculation in salt and bread and meat runs riot in defiance of the thunders of the pulpit, and executive interference and the horrors of threatened famine." In 1864, the Government found that quantities of grain paid in under the tax as newgrown were mildewed. It was grain of the previous year which speculators had held too long and now palmed off on the Government to supply the army.

Amid these desperate conditions the fate of soldiers' families became everywhere a tragedy. Unless the soldier was a land-owner his family was all but helpless. With a depreciated currency and exaggerated prices, his pay, whatever his rank, was too little to count in providing for his dependents. Local charity, dealt out by state and county boards, by relief associations, and by the generosity of neighbors, formed the barrier between his family and starvation. The landless soldier, with a family at home in desperate straits, is too often overlooked when unimaginative people heap up the statistics of "desertion" in the latter half of the war.

It was in this period, too, that amid the terrible shrinkage of the defensive lines "refugeeing" became a feature of Southern life. From the districts over which the waves of war rolled back and forth helpless families — women, children, slaves — found precarious safety together with great hardship by withdrawing to remote places which invasion was little likely to reach. An Odyssey of hard travel, often by night and half secret, is part of the war tradition of thousands of Southern families. And here, as always, the heroic women, smiling, indomitable, are the center of the picture. Their flight to preserve the children was no small test of courage. Almost invariably they had to traverse desolate country, with few attendants, through forests, and across rivers, where the arm of the law was now powerless to protect them.

Outlaws, defiant of the authorities both civil and military, — ruthless men of whom we shall hear again, — roved those great unoccupied spaces so characteristic of the Southern countryside. Many a family legend preserves still the sense of breathless caution, of pilgrimage in the night-time intently silent for fear of these masterless men. When the remote rendezvous had been reached, there a colony of refugees drew together in a steadfast despair, unprotected by their own fighting men. What strange sad pages in the history of American valor were filled by these women outwardly calm, their children romping after butterflies in a glory of sunshine, while horrid tales drifted in of deeds done by the masterless men in the forest just beyond the horizon, and far off on the soul's horizon fathers, husbands, brothers, held grimly the lines of last defense!

CHAPTER VII

THE TURNING OF THE TIDE

THE buoyancy of the Southern temper withstood the shock of Gettysburg and was not overcome by the fall of Vicksburg. Of the far-reaching significance of the latter catastrophe in particular there was little immediate recognition. Even Seddon, the Secretary of War, in November, reported that "the communication with the Trans-Mississippi, while rendered somewhat precarious and insecure, is found by no means cut off or even seriously endangered." His report was the same sort of thing as those announcements of "strategic retreats" with which the world has since become familiar. He even went so far as to argue that on the whole the South had gained rather than lost; that the control of the river was of no real value to the North; that the loss of Vicksburg "has on our side liberated for general operations in the field a large army, while it requires the enemy to maintain

cooped up, inactive, in positions insalubrious to
their soldiers, considerable detachments of their
forces."

Seddon attempted to reverse the facts, to show
that the importance of the Mississippi in commerce
was a Northern not a Southern concern. He threw
light upon the tactics of the time by his description of the future action of Confederate sharp-
shooters who were to terrorize such commercial
crews as might attempt to navigate the river; he
also told how light batteries might move swiftly
along the banks and, at points commanding the
channel, rain on the passing steamer unheralded
destruction. He was silent upon the really serious
matter, the patrol of the river by Federal gunboats
which rendered commerce with the Trans-Mississippi all but impossible.

This report, dated the 26th of November, gives a
roseate view of the war in Tennessee and enlarges
upon that dreadful battle of Chickamauga which
"ranks as one of the grandest victories of the war."
But even as the report was signed, Bragg was in
full retreat after his great disaster at Chattanooga.
On the 30th of November the Administration at
Richmond received from him a dispatch that
closed with these words: "I deem it due to the

8

cause and to myself to ask for relief from command and an investigation into the causes of the defeat." In the middle of December, Joseph E. Johnston was appointed to succeed him.

Whatever had been the illusions of the Government, they were now at an end. There was no denying that the war had entered a new stage and that the odds were grimly against the South. Davis recognized the gravity of the situation, and in his message to Congress in December, 1863, he admitted that the Trans-Mississippi was practically isolated. This was indeed a great catastrophe, for hereafter neither men nor supplies could be drawn from the far Southwest. Furthermore, the Confederacy had now lost its former precious advantage of using Mexico as a means of secret trade with Europe.

These distressing events of the four months between Vicksburg and Chattanooga established also the semi-isolation of the middle region of the lower South. The two States of Mississippi and Alabama entered upon the most desperate chapter of their history. Neither in nor out of the Confederacy, neither protected by the Confederate lines nor policed by the enemy, they were subject at once to the full rigor of the financial and military demands of the Administration of Richmond and to the full ruthlessness of plundering raids from the North. Nowhere can the contrast between the warfare of that day and the best methods of our own time be observed more clearly than in this unhappy region. At the opening of 1864 the effective Confederate lines drew an irregular zigzag across the map from a point in northern Georgia not far below Chattanooga to Mobile. Though small Confederate commands still operated bravely west of this line, the whole of Mississippi and a large part of Alabama were beyond aid from Richmond. But the average man did not grasp the situation. When a region is dominated by mobile armies the appearance of things to the civilian is deceptive. Because the powerful Federal armies of the Southwest, at the opening of 1864, were massed at strategic points from Tennessee to the Gulf, and were not extended along an obvious trench line, every brave civilian would still keep up his hope and would still insist that the middle Gulf country was far from subjugation, that its defense against the invader had not become hopeless.

Under such conditions, when the Government at Richmond called upon the men of the Southwest to regard themselves as mere sources of supply, human and otherwise, mere feeders to a theater of war that did not include their homes, it was altogether natural that they should resent the demand. All the tragic confusion that was destined in the course of the fateful year 1864 to paralyze the Government at Richmond was already apparent in the middle Gulf country when the year began. Chief among these was the inability of the State and Confederate Governments to coöperate adequately in the business of conscription. The two powers were determined rivals struggling each to seize the major part of the manhood of the community. While Richmond, looking on the situation with the eye of pure strategy, wished to draw together the full man-power of the South in one great unit, the local authorities were bent on retaining a large part of it for home defense.

In the Alabama newspapers of the latter half of 1863 strange incidents are to be found throwing light on the administrative duel. The writ of *habeas corpus*, as was so often the case in Confederate history, was the bone of contention. We have seen that the second statute empowering the President to proclaim martial law and to suspend the operation of the writ had expired by limitation in February, 1863. The Alabama courts were theoretically in full operation, but while the law was in force the military authorities had acquired a habit of arbitrary control. Though warned from Richmond in general orders that they must not take unto themselves a power vested in the President alone, they continued their previous course of action. It thereupon became necessary to issue further general orders annulling "all proclamations of martial law by general officers and others" not invested by law with adequate authority.

Neither general orders nor the expiration of the statute, however, seemed able to put an end to the interference with the local courts on the part of local commanders. The evil apparently grew during 1863. A picturesque instance is recorded with extreme fullness by the *Southern Advertiser* in the autumn of the year. In the minutely circumstantial account, we catch glimpses of one Rhodes moving heaven and earth to prove himself exempt from military service. After Rhodes is enrolled by the officers of the local military rendezvous, the sheriff attempts to turn the tables by arresting the Colonel in command. The soldiers rush to defend their Colonel, who is ill in bed at a house some distance away. The judge who had issued the writ is hot with anger at this military interference in civil affairs. Thereupon the soldiers seize him, but later, recognizing for some unexplained reason the majesty of the civil law, they release him. And the hot-tempered incident closes with the Colonel's determination to carry the case to the Supreme Court of the State.

The much harassed people of Alabama had still other causes of complaint during this same year. Again the newspapers illumine the situation. In the troubled autumn, Joseph Wheeler swept across the northern counties of Alabama and in a daring ride, with Federal cavalry hot on his trail, reached safety beyond the Tennessee River. Here his pursuers turned back and, as their horses had been broken by the swiftness of the pursuit, returning slowly, they "gleaned the country" to replace their supplies. Incidentally they pounced upon the town of Huntsville. "Their appearance here," writes a local correspondent, "was so sudden and . . . the contradictory reports of their whereabouts" had been so baffling that the townspeople had found no time to secrete things. The whole neighborhood was swept clean of cattle and almost clean of provision. "We have not enough left," the report continues, "to haul and plow with . . .

and milch cows are *non est*." Including "Stanley's big raid in July," this was the twenty-first raid which Huntsville had endured that year. The report closes with a bitter denunciation of the people of southern Alabama who as yet do not know what war means, who are accused of complete hardness of heart towards their suffering fellowcountrymen and of caring only to make money out of war prices.

When Davis sent his message to the Southern Congress at the opening of the session of 1864, the desperate plight of the middle Gulf country was at once a warning and a menace to the Government. If the conditions of that debatable land should extend eastward, there could be little doubt that the day of the Confederacy was nearing its close. To remedy the situation west of the main Confederate line, to prevent the growth of a similar condition east of it, Davis urged Congress to revive the statute permitting martial law and the suspension of the writ of *habeas corpus*. The President told Congress that in parts of the Confederacy "public meetings have been held, in some of which a treasonable design is masked by a pretense of devotion of state sovereignty, and in others is openly avowed . . . a strong suspicion is entertained that secret leagues and associations are being formed. In certain localities men of no mean position do not hesitate to avow their disloyalty and hostility to our cause, and their advocacy of peace on the terms of submission and the abolition of slavery."

This suspicion on the part of the Confederate Government that it was being opposed by organized secret societies takes us back to debatable land and to the previous year. The Bureau of Conscription submitted to the Secretary of War a report from its Alabama branch relative to "a sworn secret organization known to exist and believed to have for its object the encouragement of desertion, the protection of deserters from arrest, resistance to conscription, and perhaps other designs of a still more dangerous character." To the operations of this insidious foe were attributed the shifting of the vote in the Alabama elections, the defeat of certain candidates favored by the Government, and the return in their stead of new men "not publicly known." The suspicions of the Government were destined to further verification in the course of 1864 by the unearthing of a treasonable secret society in southwestern Virginia, the members of which were "bound to each other for the prosecution of their nefarious designs by the most solemn oaths. They were under obligation to encourage desertions from the army, and to pass and harbor all deserters, escaped prisoners, or spies; to give information to the enemy of the movements of our troops, of exposed or weakened positions, of inviting opportunities of attack, and to guide and assist the enemy either in advance or retreat." This society bore the grandiloquent name "Heroes of America" and had extended its operations into Tennessee and North Carolina.

In the course of the year further evidence was collected which satisfied the secret service of the existence of a mysterious and nameless society which had ramifications throughout Tennessee, Alabama, and Georgia. A detective who joined this "Peace Society," as it was called, for the purpose of betraying its secrets, had marvelous tales to tell of confidential information given to him by members, of how Missionary Ridge had been lost and Vicksburg had surrendered through the machinations of this society.[1]

[1] What classes were represented in these organizations it is difficult if not impossible to determine. They seem to have been involved in the singular "peace movement" which is yet to be considered. This fact gives a possible clue to the problem of their membership. A suspiciously large number of the "peace" men were original anti-

In spite of its repugnance to the suspension of the writ of *habeas corpus*, Congress was so impressed by the gravity of the situation that early in 1864 it passed another act "to suspend the privilege of the writ of *habeas corpus* in certain cases." This was not quite the same as that sweeping act of 1862 which had set the *Mercury* irrevocably in opposition. Though this act of 1864 gave the President the power to order the arrest of any person suspected of treasonable practices, and though it released military officers from all obligation to obey the order of any civil court to surrender a prisoner charged with treason, the new legislation carefully defined a list of cases in which alone this power could be lawfully used. This was the last act of the sort passed by the Confederate Congress, and when it expired by limitation ninety days after the next meeting of Congress it was not renewed.

With regard to the administration of the army, Congress can hardly be said to have met the President more than half way. The age of military service was lowered to seventeen and was raised

---

secessionists, and though many, perhaps most, of these who opposed secession became loyal servants of the Confederacy, historians may have jumped too quickly to the assumption that the sincerity of all of these men was above reproach.

to fifty. But the President was not given — though he had asked for it — general control over exemptions. Certain groups, such as ministers, editors, physicians, were in the main exempted; one overseer was exempted on each plantation where there were fifteen slaves, provided he gave bond to sell to the Government at official prices each year one hundred pounds of either beef or bacon for each slave employed and provided he would sell all his surplus produce either to the Government or to the families of soldiers. Certain civil servants of the Confederacy were also exempted as well as those whom the governors of States should "certify to be necessary for the proper administration of the State Government." The President was authorized to detail for non-military service any members of the Confederate forces "when in his judgment, justice, equity, and necessity, require such details."

This statute retained two features that had already given rise to much friction, and that were destined to be the cause of much more. It was still within the power of state governors to impede conscription very seriously. By certifying that a man was necessary to the civil administration of a State, a Governor could place him beyond the legal reach of the conscripting officers. This provision was a concession to those who looked on Davis's request for authority over exemption as the first step toward absolutism. On the other hand the statute allowed the President a free hand in the scarcely less important matter of "details." Among the imperative problems of the Confederacy, where the whole male population was needed in the public service, was the most economical separation of the two groups, the fighters and the producers. On the one hand there was the constant demand for recruits to fill up the wasted armies; on the other, the need for workers to keep the shops going and to secure the harvest. The two interests were never fully coördinated. Under the act of 1864, no farmer, mechanic, tradesman, between the ages of seventeen and fifty, if fit for military service, could remain at his work except as a "detail" under orders of the President: he might be called to the colors at a moment's notice. We shall see, presently, how the revoking of details, toward the end of what may truly be called the terrible year, was one of the major incidents of Confederate history.

Together with the new conscription act, the President approved on February 17, 1864, a reenactment of the tax in kind, with some slight concessions to the convenience of the farmers. The President's appeal for a law directly taxing slaves and land had been ignored by Congress, but another of his suggestions had been incorporated in the Funding Act. The state of the currency was now so grave that Davis attributed to it all the evils growing out of the attempts to enforce impressment. As the value of the paper dollar had by this time shrunk to six cents in specie and the volume of Confederate paper was upward of seven hundred millions, Congress undertook to reduce the volume and raise the value by compelling holders of notes to exchange them for bonds. By way of driving the note-holders to consent to the exchange, provision was made for the speedy taxation of notes for one-third their face value.

Such were the main items of the government program for 1864. Armed with this, Davis braced himself for the great task of making head against the enemies that now surrounded the Confederacy. It is an axiom of military science that when one combatant possesses the interior line, the other can offset this advantage only by exerting coincident pressure all round, thus preventing him from shifting his forces from one front to

another.   On this principle, the Northern strate-
gists had at last completed their gigantic plan for
a general envelopment of the whole Confederate
defense both by land and sea.   Grant opened
operations by crossing the Rapidan and telegraph-
ing Sherman to advance into Georgia.

The stern events of the spring of 1864 form such
a famous page in military history that the sober
civil story of those months appears by comparison
lame and impotent.   Nevertheless, the Confederate Government during those months was at
least equal to its chief obligation: it supplied and
recruited the armies.   With Grant checked at
Cold Harbor, in June, and Sherman still unable to
pierce the western line, the hopes of the Confederates were high.

In the North there was corresponding gloom.
This was the moment when all Northern opponents of the war drew together in their last attempt
to shatter the Lincoln Government and make
peace with the Confederacy.   The value to the
Southern cause of this Northern movement for
peace at any price was keenly appreciated at Richmond.   Trusted agents of the Confederacy were
even then in Canada working deftly to influence
Northern sentiment.   The negotiations with those

Northern secret societies which befriended the South belong properly in the story of Northern politics and the presidential election of 1864. They were skillfully conducted chiefly by Jacob Thompson and C. C. Clay. The reports of these agents throughout the spring and summer were all hopeful and told of "many intelligent men from the United States" who sought them out in Canada for political consultations. They discussed "our true friends from the Chicago (Democratic) convention" and even gave names of those who, they were assured, would have seats in McClellan's Cabinet. They were really not well informed upon Northern affairs, and even after the tide had turned against the Democrats in September, they were still priding themselves on their diplomatic achievement, still confident they had helped organize a great political power, had "given a stronger impetus to the peace party of the North than all other causes combined, and had greatly reduced the strength of the war party."

While Clay and Thompson built their house of cards in Canada, the Richmond Government bent anxious eyes on the western battle front. Sherman, though repulsed in his one frontal attack at Kenesaw Mountain, had steadily worked his way by the left flank of the Confederate army, until in early July he was within six miles of Atlanta. All the lower South was a-tremble with apprehension. Deputations were sent to Richmond imploring the removal of Johnston from the western command. What had he done since his appointment in December but retreat? Such was the tenor of public opinion. "It is all very well to talk of Fabian policy," said one of his detractors long afterward, "and now we can see we were rash to say the least. But at the time, all of us went wrong together. Everybody clamored for Johnston's removal." Johnston and Davis were not friends; but the President hesitated long before acting. And yet, with each day, political as well as military necessity grew more imperative. Both at Washington and Richmond the effect that the fighting in Georgia had on Northern opinion was seen to be of the first importance. Sherman was staking everything to break the Confederate line and take Atlanta. He knew that a great victory would have incalculable effect on the Northern election. Davis knew equally well that the defeat of Sherman would greatly encourage the peace party in the North. But he had no general of undoubted genius whom he could put in Johnston's place. However, the necessity for a bold stroke was so undeniable, and Johnston appeared so resolute to continue his Fabian policy, that Davis reluctantly took a desperate chance and superseded him by Hood.

During August, though the Democratic convention at Chicago drew up its platform favoring peace at any price, the anxiety of the Southern President did not abate his activities. The safety of the western line was now his absorbing concern. And in mid-August that line was turned, in a way, by Farragut's capture of Mobile Bay. As the month closed, Sherman, despite the furious blows delivered by Hood, was plainly getting the upper hand. North and South, men watched that tremendous duel with the feeling that the foundations of things were rocking. At last, on the 2d of September, Sherman, victorious, entered Atlanta.

9

CHAPTER VIII

A GAME OF CHANCE

WITH dramatic completeness in the summer and autumn of 1864, the foundations of the Confederate hope one after another gave way. Among the causes of this catastrophe was the failure of the second great attempt on the part of the Confederacy to secure recognition abroad. The subject takes us back to the latter days of 1862, when the center of gravity in foreign affairs had shifted from London to Paris. Napoleon III, at the height of his strange career, playing half a dozen dubious games at once, took up a new pastime and played at intrigue with the Confederacy. In October he accorded a most gracious interview to Slidell. He remarked that his sympathies were entirely with the South but added that, if he acted alone, England might trip him up. He spoke of his scheme for joint intervention by England, France, and Russia. Then he asked why we had

not created a navy. Slidell snapped at the bait.
He said that the Confederates would be glad to
build ships in France, that "if the Emperor would
give only some kind of verbal assurance that the
police would not observe too closely when we
wished to put on guns and men we would gladly
avail ourselves of it." To this, the imperial trick-
ster replied, "Why could you not have them built
as for the Italian Government? I do not think it
would be difficult but will consult the Minister of
Marine about it."

Slidell left the Emperor's presence confident
that things would happen. And they did. First
came Napoleon's proposal of intervention, which
was declined before the end of the year by England
and Russia. Then came his futile overtures to the
Government at Washington, his offer of mediation
— which was rejected early in 1863. But Slidell
remained confident that something else would
happen. And in this expectation also he was not
disappointed. The Emperor was deeply involved
in Mexico and was busily intriguing throughout
Europe. This was the time when Erlanger, standing high in the favor of the Emperor, made his
gambler's proposal to the Confederate authorities
about cotton. Another of the Emperor's friends

now enters the play.   On January 7, 1863, M. Arman, of Bordeaux, "the largest shipbuilder in
France," had called on the Confederate commissioner: M. Arman would be happy to build
ironclad ships for the Confederacy, and as to paying for them, cotton bonds might do the trick.

No wonder Slidell was elated, so much so that
he seems to have given little heed to the Emperor's
sinister intimation that the whole affair must be
subterranean.   But the wily Bonaparte had not
forgotten that six months earlier he had issued a
decree of neutrality forbidding Frenchmen to take
commissions from either belligerent "for the ar-
mament of vessels of war or to accept letters of
marque, or to coöperate in any way whatsoever in
the equipment or arming of any vessel of war or cor-
sair of either belligerent."   He did not intend to
abandon publicly this cautious attitude — at least,
not for the present.   And while Slidell at Paris was
completely taken in, the cooler head of A. Dudley
Mann, Confederate commissioner at Brussels, saw
what an international quicksand was the favor of
Napoleon.   It was about this time that Napoleon,
having dispatched General Forey with a fresh army
to Mexico, wrote the famous letter which gave
notice to the world of what he was about.   Mann

wrote home in alarm that the Emperor might be expected to attempt recovering Mexico's ancient areas including Texas. Slidell saw in the Forey letter only "views . . . which will not be gratifying to the Washington Government."

The adroit Arman, acting on hints from high officers of the Government, applied for permission to build and arm ships of war, alleging that he intended to send them to the Pacific and sell them to either China or Japan. To such a laudable expression of commercial enterprise, one of his fellows in the imperial ring, equipped with proper authority under Bonaparte, hastened to give official approbation, and Erlanger came forward by way of financial backer. There were conferences of Confederate agents; contracts were signed; plans were agreed upon; and the work was begun.

There was no more hopeful man in the Confederate service than Slidell when, in the full flush of pride after Chancellorsville, he appealed to the Emperor to cease waiting on other powers and recognize the Confederacy. Napoleon accorded another gracious interview but still insisted that it was impossible for him to act alone. He said that he was "more fully convinced than ever of the propriety of a general recognition by the European powers of the Confederate States but that the commerce of France and the interests of the Mexican expedition would be jeopardized by a rupture with the United States" and unless England would stand by him he dared not risk such an eventuality. In point of fact, he was like a speculator who is "hedging" on the stock exchange, both buying and selling, and trying to make up his mind on which cast to stake his fortune. At the same time he threw out once more the sinister caution about the ships. He said that the ships might be built in France but that their destination must be concealed.

That Napoleon's choice just then, if England had supported him, would have been recognition of the Confederacy, cannot be doubted. The tangle of intrigue which he called his foreign policy was not encouraging. He was deeply involved in Italian politics, where the daring of Garibaldi had reopened the struggle between clericals and liberals. In France itself the struggle between parties was keen. Here, as in the American imbroglio, he found it hard to decide with which party to break. The chimerical scheme of a Latin empire in Mexico was his spectacular device to catch the imagination, and incidentally the pocketbook, of everybody. But in order to carry out this enterprise he must be able to avert or withstand the certain hostility of the United States. Therefore, as he told Slidell, "no other power than England possessed a sufficient navy" to pull his chestnuts out of the fire. The moment was auspicious, for there was a revival of the "Southern party" in England. The sailing of the *Alabama* from Liverpool during the previous summer had encouraged the Confederate agents and their British friends to undertake further shipbuilding.

While M. Arman was at work in France, the Laird Brothers were at work in England and their dockyards contained two ironclad rams supposed to outclass any vessels of the United States navy. Though every effort had been made to keep secret the ultimate destination of these rams, the vigilance of the United States minister, reinforced by the zeal of the "Northern party," detected strong circumstantial evidence pointing toward a Confederate contract with the Lairds. A popular agitation ensued along with demands upon the Government to investigate. To mask the purposes of the Lairds, Captain James Bullock, the able special agent of the Confederate navy, was forced to fall back upon the same tactics that were being used across the Channel, and to sell the rams, on paper, to a firm in France. Neither he nor Slidell yet appreciated what a doubtful refuge was the shadow of Napoleon's wing.

Nevertheless the British Government, by this time practically alined with the North, continued its search for the real owner of the Laird rams. The "Southern party," however, had not quite given up hope, and the agitation to prevent the sailing of the rams was a keen spur to its flagging zeal. Furthermore the prestige of Lee never was higher than it was in June, 1863, when the news of Chancellorsville was still fresh and resounding in every mind. It had given new life to the Confederate hope: Lee would take Washington before the end of the summer; the Laird rams would go to sea; the Union would be driven to the wall. So reasoned the ardent friends of the South. But one thing was lacking — a European alliance. What a time for England to intervene!

While Slidell was talking with the Emperor, he had in his pocket a letter from J. A. Roebuck, an English politician who wished to force the issue in the House of Commons. As a preliminary to moving the recognition of the Confederacy, he wanted authority to deny a rumor going the rounds in London, to the effect that Napoleon had taken position against intervention. Napoleon, when he had seen the letter, began a negotiation of some sort with this politician. It is needless to enter into the complications that ensued, the subsequent recriminations, and the question as to just what Napoleon promised at this time and how many of his promises he broke. He was a diplomat of the old school, the school of lying as a fine art. He permitted Roebuck to come over to Paris for an audience, and Roebuck went away with the impression that Napoleon could be relied upon to back up a new movement for recognition. When, however, Roebuck brought the matter before the Commons at the end of the month and encountered an opposition from the Government that seemed to imply an understanding with Napoleon which was different from his own, he withdrew his motion (in July). Once more the scale turned against the Confederacy, and Gettysburg was supplemented by the seizure of the Laird rams by the British authorities. These events explain the bitter turn given to Confederate feeling toward England in the latter part of 1863. On the 4th of August Benjamin wrote to Mason that "the perusal of the recent debates in Parliament satisfies the President" that Mason's

"continued residence in London is neither con-
ducive to the interests nor consistent with the
dignity of this government," and directed him to
withdraw to Paris.

Confederate feeling, as it cooled toward England,
warmed toward France. Napoleon's Mexican
scheme, including the offer of a ready-made imperial crown to Maximilian, the brother of the
Emperor of Austria, was fully understood at Richmond; and with Napoleon's need of an American
ally, Southern hope revived. It was further
strengthened by a pamphlet which was translated
and distributed in the South as a newspaper article
under the title *France, Mexico, and the Confederate
States*. The reputed author, Michel Chevalier,
was an imperial senator, another member of the
Napoleon ring, and highly trusted by his shifty
master. The pamphlet, which emphasized the
importance of Southern independence as a condition of Napoleon's "beneficent aims" in Mexico,
was held to have been inspired, and the imperial denial was regarded as a mere matter of
form.

What appeared to be significant of the temper of
the Imperial Government was a decree of a French
court in the case of certain merchants who sought

to recover insurance on wine dispatched to America and destroyed in a ship taken by the *Alabama*. Their plea was that they were insured against loss by "pirates." The court dismissed their suit and assessed costs against them. Further evidence of Napoleon's favor was the permission given to the Confederate cruiser *Florida* to repair at Brest and even to make use of the imperial dockyard. The very general faith in Napoleon's promises was expressed by Davis in his message to Congress in December: "Although preferring our own government and institutions to those of other countries, we can have no disposition to contest the exercise by them of the same right of self-government which we assert for ourselves. If the Mexican people prefer a monarchy to a republic, it is our plain duty cheerfully to acquiesce in their decision and to evince a sincere and friendly interest in their prosperity. . . . The Emperor of the French has solemnly disclaimed any purpose to impose on Mexico a form of government not acceptable to the nation. . . ." In January, 1864, hope of recognition through support of Napoleon's Mexican policy moved the Confederate Congress to adopt resolutions providing for a Minister to the Mexican Empire and giving him instructions with

regard to a presumptive treaty. To the new post
Davis appointed General William Preston.

But what, while hope was springing high in
America, was taking place in France? So far as
the world could say, there was little if anything to
disturb the Confederates; and yet, on the horizon,
a cloud the size of a man's hand had appeared.
M. Arman had turned to another member of the
Legislative Assembly, a sound Bonapartist like
himself, M. Voruz, of Nantes, to whom he had
sublet a part of the Confederate contract. The
truth about the ships and their destination thus
became part of the archives of the Voruz firm. No
phase of Napoleonic intrigue could go very far
without encountering dishonesty, and to the confidential clerk of M. Voruz there occurred the
bright idea of doing something for himself with
this valuable diplomatic information. One fine
day the clerk was missing and with him certain
papers. Then there ensued a period of months
during which the firm and their employers could
only conjecture the full extent of their loss.

In reality, from the Confederate point of view,
everything was lost. Again the episode becomes
too complex to be followed in detail. Suffice it to
say that the papers were sold to the United States;

that the secret was exposed; that the United States made a determined assault upon the Imperial Government. In the midst of this entanglement, Slidell lost his head, for hope deferred when apparently within reach of its end is a dangerous councilor of state. In his extreme anxiety, Slidell sent to the Emperor a note the blunt rashness of which the writer could not have appreciated. Saying that he feared the Emperor's subordinates might play into the hands of Washington, he threw his fat in the fire by speaking of the ships as "now being constructed at Bordeaux and Nantes for the government of the Confederate States" and virtually claimed of Napoleon a promise to let them go to sea. Three days later the Minister of Foreign Affairs took him sharply to task because of this note, reminding him that "what had passed with the Emperor was confidential" and dropping the significant hint that France could not be forced into war by "indirection." According to Slidell's version of the interview "the Minister's tone changed completely" when Slidell replied with "a detailed history of the affair showing that the idea originated with the Emperor." Perhaps the Minister knew more than he chose to betray.

From this hour the game was up. Napoleon's purpose all along seems to have been quite plain. He meant to help the South to win by itself, and, after it had won, to use it for his own advantage. So precarious was his position in Europe that he dared not risk an American war without England's aid, and England had cast the die. In this way, secrecy was the condition necessary to continued building of the ships. Now that the secret was out, Napoleon began to shift his ground. He sounded the Washington Government and found it suspiciously equivocal as to Mexico. To silence the French republicans, to whom the American minister had supplied information about the ships, Napoleon tried at first muzzling the press. But as late as February, 1864, he was still carrying water on both shoulders. His Minister of Marine notified the builders that they must get the ships out of France, unarmed, under fictitious sale to some neutral country. The next month, reports which the Confederate commissioners sent home became distinctly alarming. Mann wrote from Brussels: "Napoleon has enjoined upon Maximilian to hold no official relations with our commissioners in Mexico." Shortly after this Slidell received a shock that was the beginning of the end: Maximilian, on passing through Paris on his way to Mexico, refused to receive him.

The Mexican project was now being condemned by all classes in France. Nevertheless, the Government was trying to float a Mexican loan, and it is hardly fanciful to think that on this loan the last hope of the Confederacy turned. Despite the popular attitude toward Mexico, the loan was going well when the House of Representatives of the United States dealt the Confederacy a staggering blow. It passed unanimous resolutions in the most grim terms, denouncing the substitution of monarchical for republican government in Mexico under European auspices. When this action was reported in France, the Mexican loan collapsed.

Napoleon's Italian policy was now moving rapidly toward the crisis which it reached during the following summer when he surrendered to the opposition and promised to withdraw the French troops from Rome. In May, when the loan collapsed, there was nothing for it but to throw over his dear friends of the Confederacy. Presently he had summoned Arman before him, "rated him severely," and ordered him to make *bona fide* sales of the ships to neutral powers. The Minister of Marine professed surprise and indignation at

Arman's trifling with the neutrality of the Imperial Government.   And that practically was the end of the episode.

Equally complete was the breakdown of the Confederate negotiations with Mexico.   General Preston was refused recognition.   In those fierce days of July when the fate of Atlanta was in the balance, the pride and despair of the Confederate Government flared up in a haughty letter to Preston reminding him that "it had never been the intention of this Government to offer any arguments to the new Government of Mexico . . . nor to place itself in any attitude other than that of complete equality," and directing him to make no further overtures to the Mexican Emperor.

And then came the *débâcle* in Georgia.   On that same 20th of September when Benjamin poured out in a letter to Slidell his stored-up bitterness denouncing Napoleon, Davis, feeling the last crisis was upon him, left Richmond to join the army in Georgia.   His frame of mind he had already expressed when he said, "We have no friends abroad."

CHAPTER IX

THE loss of Atlanta was the signal for another conflict of authority within the Confederacy. Georgia was now in the condition in which Alabama had found herself in the previous year. A great mobile army of invaders lay encamped on her soil. And yet there was still a state Government established at the capital. Inevitably the man who thought of the situation from the point of view of what we should now call the general staff, and the man who thought of it from the point of view of a citizen of the invaded State, suffered each an intensification of feeling, and each became determined to solve the problem in his own way. The President of the Confederacy and the Governor of Georgia represented these incompatible points of view.

The Governor, Joseph E. Brown, is one of the puzzling figures of Confederate history. We have already encountered him as a dogged opponent of the Administration.   With the whole fabric of Southern life toppling about his ears, Brown argued, quibbled, evaded, and became a rallying-point of disaffection.   That more eminent Georgian, Howell Cobb, applied to him very severe language, and they became engaged in a controversy over that provision of the Conscription Act which exempted state officials from military service.   While the Governor of Virginia was refusing certificates of exemption to the minor civil officers such as justices of the peace, Brown by proclamation promised his "protection" to the most insignificant civil servants.   "Will even your Excellency," demanded Cobb, "certify that in any county of Georgia twenty justices of the peace and an equal number of constables are necessary for the proper administration of the state government?"   The Bureau of Conscription estimated that Brown kept out of the army approximately 8000 eligible men.   The truth seems to be that neither by education nor heredity was this Governor equipped to conceive large ideas.   He never seemed conscious of the war as a whole, or of the Confederacy as a whole. To defend Georgia and, if that could not be done, to make peace for Georgia — such in the mind of Brown was the aim of the war.   His restless

HOWELL COBB

Wood engraving from a photograph, lent by General Marcus J. Wright, published in *Abraham Lincoln, A History*, by Nicolay and Hay. The Century Company, New York, 1904.

Gravure, Anderson-Lamb Co. N.Y.

jealousy of the Administration finds its explanation in his fear that it would denude his State of men. The seriousness of Governor Brown's opposition became apparent within a week of the fall of Atlanta. Among Hood's forces were some 10,000 Georgia militia. Brown notified Hood that these troops had been called out solely with a view to the defense of Atlanta, that since Atlanta had been lost they must now be permitted "to return to their homes and look for a time after important interests," and that therefore he did "withdraw said organizations" from Hood's command. In other words, Brown was afraid that they might be taken out of the State. By proclamation he therefore gave the militia a furlough of thirty days. Previous to the issue of this proclamation, Seddon had written to Brown making requisition for his 10,000 militia to assist in a pending campaign against Sherman. Two days after his proclamation had appeared, Brown, in a voluminous letter full of blustering rhetoric and abounding in sneers at the President, demanded immediate reinforcements by order of the President and threatened that, if they were not sent, he would recall the Georgia troops from the army of Lee and would command "all the sons of Georgia to return to their own State and within their own limits to rally round her glorious flag."

So threatening was the situation in Georgia that Davis attempted to take it into his own hands. In a grim frame of mind he left Richmond for the front. The resulting military arrangements do not of course belong strictly to the subject-matter of this volume; but the brief tour of speechmaking which Davis made in Georgia and the interior of South Carolina must be noticed; for his purpose seems to have been to put the military point of view squarely before the people. He meant them to see how the soldier looked at the situation, ignoring all demands of locality, of affiliation, of hardship, and considering only how to meet and beat the enemy. In his tense mood he was not always fortunate in his expressions. At Augusta, for example, he described Beauregard, whom he had recently placed in general command over Georgia and South Carolina, as one who would do whatever the President told him to do. But this idea of military self-effacement was not happily worded, and the enemies of Davis seized on his phraseology as further evidence of his instinctive autocracy. The *Mercury* compared him to the Emperor of Russia and declared the tactless remark to be "as

insulting to General Beauregard as it is false and
presumptuous in the President."

Meanwhile Beauregard was negotiating with
Brown. Though they came to an understanding
about the disposition of the militia, Brown still
tried to keep control of the state troops. When
Sherman was burning Atlanta preparatory to the
March to the Sea, Brown addressed to the Secretary of War another interminable epistle, denouncing the Confederate authorities and asserting his
willingness to fight both the South and the North
if they did not both cease invading his rights. But
the people of Georgia were better balanced than
their Governor. Under the leadership of such men
as Cobb they rose to the occasion and did their
part in what proved a vain attempt to conduct a
"people's war." Their delegation at Richmond
sent out a stirring appeal assuring them that Davis
was doing for them all it was possible to do. "Let
every man fly to arms," said the appeal. "Remove your negroes, horses, cattle, and provisions
from before Sherman's army, and burn what you
cannot carry. Burn all bridges and block up the
roads in his route. Assail the invader in front,
flank, and rear, by night and by day. Let him
have no rest."

The Richmond Government was unable to detach any considerable force from the northern front. Its contribution to the forces in Georgia was accomplished by such pathetic means as a general order calling to the colors all soldiers furloughed or in hospital, "except those unable to travel"; by revoking all exemptions to farmers, planters, and mechanics, except munitions workers; and by placing one-fifth of the ordnance and mining bureau in the battle service.

All the world knows how futile were these endeavors to stop the whirlwind of desolation that was Sherman's march. He spent his Christmas Day in Savannah. Then the center of gravity shifted from Georgia to South Carolina. Throughout the two desperate months that closed 1864 the authorities of South Carolina had vainly sought for help from Richmond. Twice the Governor made official request for the return to South Carolina of some of her own troops who were at the front in Virginia. Davis first evaded and then refused the request. Lee had informed him that if the forces on the northern front were reduced, the evacuation of Richmond would become inevitable.

The South Carolina Government, in December, 1864, seems to have concluded that the State must save itself. A State Conscription Act was passed placing all white males between the ages of sixteen and sixty at the disposal of the state authorities for emergency duty. An Exemption Act set forth a long list of persons who should not be liable to conscription by the Confederate Government. Still a third act regulated the impressment of slaves for work on fortifications so as to enable the state authorities to hold a check upon the Confederate authorities. The significance of the three statutes was interpreted by a South Carolina soldier, General John S. Preston, in a letter to the Secretary of War that was a wail of despair. "This legislation is an explicit declaration that this State does not intend to contribute another soldier or slave to the public defense, except on such terms as may be dictated by her authorities. The example will speedily be followed by North Carolina and Georgia, the Executives of those States having already assumed the position."

The division between the two parties in South Carolina had now become bitter. To Preston the men behind the State Exemption Act appeared as "designing knaves." The *Mercury*, on the other hand, was never more relentless toward Davis than in the winter of 1864–1865. However, none or almost none of the anti-Davis men in South Carolina made the least suggestion of giving up the struggle. To fight to the end but also to act as a check upon the central Government — as the new Governor, Andrew G. Magrath, said in his inaugural address in December, 1864, — was the aim of the dominant party in South Carolina. How far the State Government and the Confederate Government had drifted apart is shown by two comments which were made in January, 1865. Lee complained that the South Carolina regiments, "much reduced by hard service," were not being recruited up to their proper strength because of the measures adopted in the southeastern States to retain conscripts at home. About the same date the *Mercury* arraigned Davis for leaving South Carolina defenseless in the face of Sherman's coming offensive, and asked whether Davis intended to surrender the Confederacy.

And in the midst of this critical period, the labor problem pushed to the fore again. The revocation of industrial details, necessary as it was, had put almost the whole male population — in theory, at least — in the general Confederate army. How far-reaching was the effect of this order may be judged from the experience of the Columbia and

Augusta Railroad Company. This road was building through the interior of the State a new line which was rendered imperatively necessary by Sherman's seizure of the lines terminating at Savannah. The effect of the revocation order on the work in progress was described by the president of the road in a letter to the Secretary of War:

In July and August I made a fair beginning and by October we had about 600 hands. General Order No. 77 took off many of our contractors and hands. We still had increased the number of hands to about 400 when Sherman started from Atlanta. The military authorities of Augusta took about 300 of them to fortify that city. These contractors being from Georgia returned with their slaves to their homes after being discharged at Augusta. We still have between 500 and 600 hands at work and are adding to the force every week.

The great difficulty has been in getting contractors exempt or definitely detailed since Order No. 77. I have not exceeded eight or nine contractors now detailed. The rest are exempt from other causes or over age.

It was against such a background of economic confusion that Magrath wrote to the Governor of North Carolina making a revolutionary proposal. Virtually admitting that the Confederacy had been shattered, and knowing the disposition of those in authority to see only the military aspects of any given situation, he prophesied two things: that the generals would soon attempt to withdraw Lee's army south of Virginia, and that the Virginia troops in that army would refuse to go. "It is natural under the circumstances," said he, "that they would not." He would prepare for this emergency by an agreement among the Southeastern and Gulf States to act together irrespective of Richmond, and would thus weld the military power of these States into "a compact and organized mass."

Governor Vance, with unconscious subtlety, etched a portrait of his own mind when he replied that the crisis demanded "particularly the skill of the politician perhaps more than that of the great general." He adroitly evaded saying what he really thought of the situation but he made two explicit counter-proposals. He suggested that a demand should be made for the restoration of General Johnston and for the appointment of General Lee to "full and absolute command of all the forces of the Confederacy." On the day on which Vance wrote to Magrath, the *Mercury* lifted up its voice and cried out for a Lee to take charge of the Government and save the Confederacy. About the same time Cobb wrote to Davis in the most friendly way, warning him that he had scarcely a supporter left in Georgia and that, in view of the great popular reaction in favor of Johnston, concessions to the opposition were an imperative necessity. "By accident," said he, "I have become possessed of the facts in connection with the proposed action of the Governors of certain States." He disavowed any sympathy with the movement but warned Davis that it was a serious menace.

Two other intrigues added to the general political confusion. One of these, the "Peace Movement," will be considered in the next chapter. The other was closely connected with the alleged conspiracy to depose Davis and set up Lee as dictator. If the traditional story, accepted by able historians, may be believed, William C. Rives, of the Confederate Congress, carried in January, 1865, to Lee from a congressional cabal an invitation to accept the rôle of Cromwell. The greatest difficulty in the way of accepting the tradition is the extreme improbability that any one who knew anything of Lee would have been so foolish as to make such a proposal. Needless to add, the tradition includes Lee's refusal to overturn the Government.

There can be no doubt, however, that all the enemies of Davis in Congress and out of it, in the opening months of 1865, made a determined series of attacks upon his Administration. Nor can there be any doubt that the popular faith in Lee was used as their trump card. To that end, a bill was introduced to create the office of commanding general of the Confederate armies. The bill was generally applauded, and every one assumed that the new office was to be given to Lee. On the day after the bill had passed the Senate the Virginia Legislature resolved that the appointment of General Lee to supreme command would "reanimate the spirit of the armies as well as the people of the several States and . . . inspire increased confidence in the final success of the cause." When the bill was sent to the President, it was accompanied by a resolution asking him to restore Johnston. While Davis was considering this bill, the Virginia delegation in the House, headed by the Speaker, Thomas S. Bocock, waited upon the President, informed him what was really wanted was a change of Cabinet, and told him that three-fourths of the House would support a resolution of want of confidence in the Cabinet. The next day Bocock repeated the demand in a note which Davis described as a "warning if not a threat."

The situation of both President and country was now desperate. The program with which the Government had entered so hopefully upon this fated year had broken down at almost every point. In addition to the military and administrative disasters, the financial and economic situation was as bad as possible. So complete was the financial breakdown that Secretary Memminger, utterly disheartened, had resigned his office, and the Treasury was now administered by a Charleston merchant, George A. Trenholm. But the financial chaos was wholly beyond his control. The government notes reckoned in gold were worth about three cents on the dollar. The Government itself avoided accepting them. It even bought up United States currency and used it in transacting the business of the army. The extent of the financial collapse was to be measured by such incidents as the following which is recounted in a report that had passed under Davis's eye only a few weeks before the "threat" of Bocock was uttered: "Those holding the four per cent certificates complain that the Government as far as possible discredits them. Fractions of hundreds cannot be paid with them. I saw a widow lady, a few days since, offer to pay her taxes of $1,271.31 with a certificate of $1,300. The tax-gatherer refused to give her the change of $28.69. She then offered the whole certificate for the taxes. This was refused. This apparent injustice touched her far more than the amount of the taxes."

A letter addressed to the President from Griffin, Georgia, contained this dreary picture:

Unless something is done and that speedily, there will be thousands of the best citizens of the State and heretofore as loyal as any in the Confederacy, that will not care one cent which army is victorious in Georgia. . . . Since August last there have been thousands of cavalry and wagon trains feeding upon our cornfields and for which our quartermasters and officers in command of trains, regiments, battalions, companies, and squads, have been giving the farmers receipts, and we were all told these receipts would pay our government taxes and tithing; and yet not one of them will be taken by our collector. . . . And yet we are threatened with having our lands sold for taxes. Our scrip for corn used by our generals will not be taken. . . . How is it that we have certified claims upon our Government, past due ten months, and when we enter the quartermaster's office we see placed up conspicuously in large letters "no funds." Some of these said quartermasters [who] four years ago were not worth the clothes upon their backs, are now large dealers in lands, negroes, and real estate.

There was almost universal complaint that government contractors were speculating in supplies and that the Impressment Law was used by officials to cover their robbery of both the Government and the people. Allowing for all the panic of the moment, one is forced to conclude that the smoke is too dense not to cover a good deal of fire. In a word, at the very time when local patriotism everywhere was drifting into opposition to the general military command and when Congress was reflecting this widespread loss of confidence, the Government was loudly charged with inability to restrain graft. In all these accusations there was much injustice. Conditions that the Government was powerless to control were cruelly exaggerated, and the motives of the Government were falsified. For all this exaggeration and falsification the press was largely to blame. Moreover, the press, at least in dangerously large proportion, was schooling the people to hold Davis personally responsible for all their suffering. General Bragg was informed in a letter from a correspondent in Mobile that "men have been taught to look upon the President as an inexorably self-willed man who will see the country to the devil before giving up an opinion or a purpose."

This deliberate fostering of an anti-Davis spirit might seem less malicious if the fact were not known that many editors detested Davis because of his desire to abolish the exemption of editors from conscription. Their ignoble course brings to mind one of the few sarcasms recorded of Lee — the remark that the great mistake of the South was in making all its best military geniuses editors of newspapers. But it must be added in all fairness that the great opposition journals, such as the *Mercury*, took up this new issue with the President because they professed to see in his attitude toward the press a determination to suppress freedom of speech, so obsessed was the opposition with the idea that Davis was a monster! Whatever explanations may be offered for the prevalence of graft, the impotence of the Government at Richmond contributed to the general demoralization. In regions like Georgia and Alabama, the Confederacy was now powerless to control its agents. Furthermore, in every effort to assume adequate control of the food situation the Government met the continuous opposition of two groups of opponents — the unscrupulous parasites and the bigots of economic and constitutional theory. Of the activities of the first group, one incident is sufficient to tell the whole story. At Richmond, in the autumn of 1864, the grocers were selling rice at two dollars and a half a pound. It happened that the Governor of Virginia was William Smith, one of the strong men of the Confederacy who has not had his due from the historians. He saw that even under the intolerable conditions of the moment this price was shockingly exorbitant. To remedy matters, the Governor took the State of Virginia into business, bought rice where it was grown, imported it, and sold it in Richmond at fifty cents a pound, with sufficient profit to cover all costs of handling.

Nevertheless, when Smith urged the Virginia Legislature to assume control of business as a temporary measure, he was at once assailed by the second group — those martinets of constitutionalism who would not give up their cherished Anglo-Saxon tradition of complete individualism in government. The Administration lost some of its stanchest supporters the moment its later organ, the *Sentinel*, began advocating the general regulation of prices. With ruin staring them in the face, these devotees of tradition could only reiterate their ancient formulas, nail their colors to the mast, and go down, satisfied that, if they failed with these principles, they would have failed still more terribly without them. Confronting the practical question how to prevent speculators from charging 400 per cent profit, these men turned grim but did not abandon their theory. In the latter part of 1864 they alined themselves with the opposition when the government commissioners of impressment fixed an official schedule that boldly and ruthlessly cut under market prices. The attitude of many such people was expressed by the *Montgomery Mail* when it said:

"The tendency of the age, the march of the American people, is toward monarchy, and unless the tide is stopped we shall reach something worse than monarchy.

"Every step we have taken during the past four years has been in the direction of military despotism.

"Half our laws are unconstitutional."

Another danger of the hour was the melting away of the Confederate army under the very eyes of its commanders. The records showed that there were 100,000 absentees. And though the wrathful officials of the Bureau of Conscription labeled them all "deserters," the term covered great numbers who had gone home to share the sufferings of their families.

Such in brief was the fateful background of the congressional attack upon the Administration in January, 1865. Secretary Seddon, himself a Virginian, believing that he was the main target of the hostility of the Virginia delegation, insisted upon resigning. Davis met this determination with firmness, not to say infatuation, and in spite of the congressional crisis, exhausted every argument to persuade Seddon to remain in office. He denied the right of Congress to control his Cabinet, but he was finally constrained to allow Seddon to retire. The bitterness inspired by these attempts to coerce the President may be gaged by a remark attributed to Mrs. Davis. Speaking of the action of Congress in forcing upon him the new plan for a single commanding general of all the armies, she is said to have exclaimed, "I think I am the proper person to advise Mr. Davis and if I were he, I would die or be hung before I would submit to the humiliation."

Nevertheless the President surrendered to Congress. On January 26, 1865, he signed the bill creating the office of commanding general and at once bestowed the office upon Lee. It must not be supposed, however, that Lee himself had the slightest sympathy with the congressional cabal which had forced upon the President this reorganization of the army. In accepting his new position he pointedly ignored Congress by remarking, "I am indebted alone to the kindness of His Excellency, the President, for my nomination to this high and arduous office."

The popular clamor for the restoration of Johnston had still to be appeased. Disliking Johnston and knowing that the opposition was using a popular general as a club with which to beat himself, Davis hesitated long but in the end yielded to the inevitable. To make the reappointment himself, however, was too humiliating. He left it to the new commander-in-chief, who speedily restored Johnston to command.

CHAPTER X

DISINTEGRATION

WHILE these factions, despite their disagreements, were making valiant efforts to carry on the war, other factions were stealthily cutting the ground from under them. There were two groups of men ripe for disaffection — original Unionists unreconciled to the Confederacy and indifferentists conscripted against their will.

History has been unduly silent about these disaffected men. At the time so real was the belief in state rights that contemporaries were reluctant to admit that any Southerner, once his State had seceded, could fail to be loyal to its commands. Nevertheless in considerable areas — such, for example, as East Tennessee — the majority remained to the end openly for the Union, and there were large regions in the South to which until quite recently the eye of the student had not been turned. They were like deep shadows under mighty trees on the face of a brilliant landscape. When the peasant Unionist who had been forced into the army deserted, however, he found in these shadows a nucleus of desperate men ready to combine with him in opposition to the local authorities.

Thus were formed local bands of free companions who pillaged the civilian population. The desperadoes whom the deserters joined have been described by Professor Dodd as the "neglected by-products" of the old régime. They were broken white men, or the children of such, of the sort that under other circumstances have congregated in the slums of great cities. Though the South lacked great cities, nevertheless it had its slum — a widespread slum, scattered among its swamps and forests. In these fastnesses were the lowest of the poor whites, in whom hatred of the dominant whites and vengeful malice against the negro burned like slow fires. When almost everywhere the countryside was stripped of its fighting men, these wretches emerged from their swamps and forests, like the Paris rabble emerging from its dens at the opening of the Revolution. But unlike the Frenchmen, they were too sodden to be capable of ideas. Like predatory wild beasts they revenged themselves upon the society that had cast them off, and with utter heartlessness they smote the now defenseless negro. In the old days, with the country well policed, the slaves had been protected against their fury, but war now changed all. The negro villages — or "streets," as the term was — were without arms and without white police within call. They were ravaged by these marauders night after night, and negroes were not the only victims, for in remote districts even murder of the whites became a familiar horror.

The antiwar factions were not necessarily, however, users of violence. There were some men who cherished a dream which they labeled "reconstruction"; and there were certain others who believed in separate state action, still clinging to the illusion that any State had it in its power to escape from war by concluding a separate peace with the United States.

Yet neither of these illusions made much headway in the States that had borne the strain of intellectual leadership. Virginia and South Carolina, though seldom seeing things eye to eye and finally drifting in opposite directions, put but little faith in either "reconstruction" or separate peace. Their leaders had learned the truth about men and nations; they knew that life is a grim business; they

knew that war had unloosed passions that had to
spend themselves and that could not be talked
away.

But there was scattered over the Confederacy a
population which lacked experience of the world
and which included in the main those small farmers
and semipeasants who under the old régime were
released from the burden of taxation and at the
same time excluded from the benefits of education.
Among these people the illusions of the higher
classes were reflected without the ballast of mentality. Ready to fight on any provocation, yet
circumscribed by their own natures, not understanding life, unable to picture to themselves
different types and conditions, these people were
as prone as children to confuse the world of their
own desire with the world of fact. When hardship
came, when taxation fell upon them with a great
blow, when the war took a turn that necessitated
imagination for its understanding and faith for its
pursuit, these people with childlike simplicity immediately became panic-stricken. Like the similar class in the North, they had measureless faith
in talk. Hence for them, as for Horace Greeley and many another, sprang up the notion that
if only all their sort could be brought together

for talk and talk and yet more talk, the Union could be "reconstructed" just as it used to be, and the cruel war would end. Before their eyes, as before Greeley in 1864, danced the fata morgana of a convention of all the States, talking, talking, talking.

The peace illusion centered in North Carolina, where the people were as enthusiastic for state sovereignty as were any Southerners. They had seceded mainly because they felt that this principle had been attacked. Having themselves little if any intention to promote slavery, they nevertheless were prompt to resent interference with the system or with any other Southern institution. Jonathan Worth said that they looked on both abolition and secession as children of the devil, and he put the responsibility for the secession of his State wholly upon Lincoln and his attempt to coerce the lower South. This attitude was probably characteristic of all classes in North Carolina. There also an unusually large percentage of men lacked education and knowledge of the world. We have seen how the first experience with taxation produced instant and violent reaction. The peasant farmers of the western counties and the general mass of the people began to distrust the planter class. They began asking if their allies, the other States, were controlled by that same class which seemed to be crushing them by the exaction of tithes. And then the popular cry was raised: Was there after all anything in the war for the masses in North Carolina? Had they left the frying-pan for the fire? Could they better things by withdrawing from association with their present allies and going back alone into the Union? The delusion that they could do so whenever they pleased and on the old footing seems to have been widespread. One of their catch phrases was "the Constitution as it is and the Union as it was." Throughout 1863, when the agitation against tithes was growing every day, the "conservatives" of North Carolina, as their leaders named them, were drawing together in a definite movement for peace. This project came to a head during the next year in those grim days when Sherman was before Atlanta. Holden, that champion of the opposition to tithes, became a candidate for Governor against Vance, who was standing for reëlection. Holden stated his platform in the organ of his party: "If the people of North Carolina are for perpetual conscriptions, impressments and seizures to keep up a perpetual, devastating and exhausting war, let them vote for Governor Vance, for he is for 'fighting it out now'; but if they believe, from the bitter experience of the last three years, that the sword can never end it, and are in favor of steps being taken by the State to urge negotiations by the general government for an honorable and speedy peace, they must vote for Mr. Holden."

As Holden, however, was beaten by a vote that stood about three to one, Governor Vance continued in power, but just what he stood for and just what his supporters understood to be his policy would be hard to say. A year earlier he was for attempting to negotiate peace, but though professing to have come over to the war party he was never a cordial supporter of the Confederacy. In a hundred ways he played upon the strong local distrust of Richmond, and upon the feeling that North Carolina was being exploited in the interests of the remainder of the South. To cripple the efficiency of Confederate conscription was one of his constant aims. Whatever his views of the struggle in which he was engaged, they did not include either an appreciation of Southern nationalism or the strategist's conception of war. Granted that the other States were merely his allies, Vance pursued a course that might justly have aroused their suspicion, for so far as he was able he devoted the resources of the State wholly to the use of its own citizens.   The food and the manufactures of North Carolina were to be used solely by its own troops, not by troops of the Confederacy raised in other States.   And yet, subsequent to his reëlection, he was not a figure in the movement to negotiate peace.

Meanwhile in Georgia, where secession had met with powerful opposition, the policies of the Government had produced discontent not only with the management of the war but with the war itself.   And now Alexander H. Stephens becomes, for a season, very nearly the central figure of Confederate history.   Early in 1864 the new act suspending the writ of *habeas corpus* had aroused the wrath of Georgia, and Stephens had become the mouthpiece of the opposition.   In an address to the Legislature, he condemned in most exaggerated language not only the *Habeas Corpus* Act but also the new Conscription Act.   Soon afterward he wrote a long letter to Herschel V. Johnson, who, like himself, had been an enemy of secession in 1861.   He said that if Johnson doubted that the *Habeas Corpus* Act was a blow struck at the very "vitals of liberty," then he "would not believe though one were to rise from the dead." In this extraordinary letter Stephens went on "most confidentially" to state his attitude toward Davis thus: "While I do not and never have regarded him as a great man or statesman on a large scale, or a man of any marked genius, yet I have regarded him as a man of good intentions, weak and vacillating, timid, petulant, peevish, obstinate, but not firm. Am now beginning to doubt his good intentions. . . . His whole policy on the organization and discipline of the army is perfectly consistent with the hypothesis that he is aiming at absolute power."

That a man of Stephens's ability should have dealt in fustian like this in the most dreadful moment of Confederate history is a psychological problem that is not easily solved. To be sure, Stephens was an extreme instance of the martinet of constitutionalism. He reminds us of those old-fashioned generals of whom Macaulay said that they preferred to lose a battle according to rule than win it by an exception. Such men find it easy to transform into a bugaboo any one who appears to them to be acting irregularly. Stephens in his own mind had so transformed the President. The enormous difficulties and the wholly

abnormal circumstances which surrounded Davis
counted with Stephens for nothing at all, and he
reasoned about the Administration as if it were
operating in a vacuum. Having come to this extraordinary position, Stephens passed easily into a
rôle that verged upon treason.[1]

Peace talk was now in the air, and especially was
there chatter about reconstruction. The illusion-
ists seemed unable to perceive that the reëlection
of Lincoln had robbed them of their last card.
These dreamers did not even pause to wonder why

[1] There can be no question that Stephens never did anything which
in his own mind was in the least disloyal. And yet it was Stephens
who, in the autumn of 1864, was singled out by artful men as a possible
figurehead in the conduct of a separate peace negotiation with Sherman. A critic very hostile to Stephens and his faction might here
raise the question as to what was at bottom the motive of Governor
Brown, in the autumn of 1864, in withdrawing the Georgia militia
from Hood's command. Was there something afoot that has never
quite revealed itself on the broad pages of history? As ordinarily
told, the story is simply that certain desperate Georgians asked
Stephens to be their ambassador to Sherman to discuss terms; that
Sherman had given them encouragement; but that Stephens avoided
the trap, and so nothing came of it. The recently published correspondence of Toombs, Stephens, and Cobb, however, contains one
passage that has rather a startling sound. Brown, writing to Stephens
regarding his letter refusing to meet Sherman, says, "It keeps the
door open and I think this is wise." At the same time he made a
public statement that "Georgia has power to act independently but
her faith is pledged by implication to her Southern sisters . . . will
triumph with her Southern sisters or sink with them in common ruin."
It is still to be discovered what "door" Stephens was supposed to have
kept open.

after the terrible successes of the Federal army in Georgia, Lincoln should be expected to reverse his policy and restore the Union with the Southern States on the old footing. The peace mania also invaded South Carolina and was espoused by one of its Congressmen, Mr. Boyce, but he made few converts among his own people. The *Mercury* scouted the idea; clear-sighted and disillusioned, it saw the only alternatives to be victory or subjugation. Boyce's argument was that the South had already succumbed to military despotism and would have to endure it forever unless it accepted the terms of the invaders. News of Boyce's attitude called forth vigorous protest from the army before Petersburg, and even went so far afield as New York, where it was discussed in the columns of the *Herald*.

In the midst of the Northern elections, when Davis was hoping great things from the anti-Lincoln men, Stephens had said in print that he believed Davis really wished the Northern peace party defeated, whereupon Davis had written to him demanding reasons for this astounding charge. To the letter, which had missed Stephens at his home and had followed him late in the year to Richmond, Stephens wrote in the middle of December a long reply which is one of the most curious documents in American history. He justified himself upon two grounds. One was a statement which Davis had made in a speech at Columbia, in October, indicating that he was averse to the scheme of certain Northern peace men for a convention of all the States. Stephens insisted that such a convention would have ended the war and secured the independence of the South. Davis cleared himself on this charge by saying that the speech at Columbia "was delivered after the publication of McClellan's letter avowing his purpose to force reunion by war if we declined reconstruction when offered, and therefore warned the people against delusive hopes of peace from any other influence than that to be exerted by the manifestation of an unconquerable spirit."

As Stephens professed to have independence and not reconstruction for his aim, he had missed his mark with this first shot. He fared still worse with the second. During the previous spring a Northern soldier captured in the southeast had appealed for parole on the ground that he was a secret emissary to the President from the peace men of the North. Davis, who did not take him seriously, gave orders to have the case investigated, but Stephens, whose mentality in this period is so curiously overcast, swallowed the prisoner's story without hesitation. He and Davis had a considerable amount of correspondence on the subject. In the fierce tension of the summer of 1864 the War Department went so far as to have the man's character investigated, but the report was unsatisfactory. He was not paroled and died in prison. This episode Stephens now brought forward as evidence that Davis had frustrated an attempt of the Northern peace party to negotiate. Davis contented himself with replying, "I make no comment on this."

The next step in the peace intrigue took place at the opening of the next year, 1865. Stephens attempted to address the Senate on his favorite topic, the wickedness of the suspension of *habeas corpus;* was halted by a point of parliamentary law; and when the Senate sustained an appeal from his decision, left the chamber in a pique. Hunter, now a Senator, became an envoy to placate him and succeeded in bringing him back. Thereupon Stephens poured out his soul in a furious attack upon the Administration. He ended by submitting resolutions which were just what he might have submitted four years earlier before a gun had been fired, so entirely had his mind crystallized in the

12

stress of war!   These resolutions, besides reasserting the full state rights theory, assumed the readiness of the North to make peace and called for a general convention of all the States to draw up some new arrangement on a confessed state rights basis.   More than a month before, Lincoln had been reëlected on an unequivocal nationalistic platform.   And yet Stephens continued to believe that the Northerners did not mean what they said and that in congregated talking lay the magic which would change the world of fact into the world of his own desire.

At this point in the peace intrigue the ambiguous figure of Napoleon the Little reappears, though only to pass ghostlike across the back of the stage. The determination of Northern leaders to oppose Napoleon had suggested to shrewd politicians a possible change of front.   That singular member of the Confederate Congress, Henry S. Foote, thought he saw in the Mexican imbroglio means to bring Lincoln to terms.   In November he had introduced into the House resolutions which intimated that "it might become the true policy of . . . the Confederate States to consent to the yielding of the great principle embodied in the Monroe Doctrine."   The House referred his resolutions to the Committee on Foreign Affairs, and there they slumbered until January.

Meanwhile a Northern politician brought on the specter of Napoleon for a different purpose. Early in January, 1865, Francis P. Blair made a journey to Richmond and proposed to Davis a plan of reconciliation involving the complete abandonment of slavery, the reunion of all the States, and an expedition against Mexico in which Davis was to play the leading rôle. Davis cautiously refrained from committing himself, though he gave Blair a letter in which he expressed his willingness to enter into negotiations for peace between "the two countries." The visit of Blair gave new impetus to the peace intrigue. The Confederate House Committee on Foreign Affairs reported resolutions favoring an attempt to negotiate with the United States so as to "bring into view" the possibility of coöperation between the United States and the Confederacy to maintain the Monroe Doctrine. The same day saw another singular incident. For some reason that has never been divulged Foote determined to counterbalance Blair's visit to Richmond by a visit of his own to Washington. In attempting to pass through the Confederate lines he was arrested by the military authorities. With this fiasco Foote passes from the stage of history.

The doings of Blair, however, continued to be a topic of general interest throughout January. The military intrigue was now simmering down through the creation of the office of commanding general. The attempt of the congressional opposition to drive the whole Cabinet from office reached a compromise in the single retirement of the Secretary of War. Before the end of the month the peace question was the paramount one before Congress and the country. Newspapers discussed the movements of Blair, apparently with little knowledge, and some of the papers asserted hopefully that peace was within reach. Cooler heads, such as the majority of the Virginia Legislature, rejected this idea as baseless. The *Mercury* called the peace party the worst enemy of the South. Lee was reported by the Richmond correspondent of the *Mercury* as not caring a fig for the peace project. Nevertheless the rumor persisted that Blair had offered peace on terms that the Confederacy could accept. Late in the month, Davis appointed Stephens, Hunter, and John A. Campbell commissioners to confer with the Northern authorities with regard to peace.

There followed the famous conference of February 3, 1865, in the cabin of a steamer at Hampton Roads, with Seward and Lincoln. The Confederate commissioners represented two points of view: that of the Administration, unwilling to make peace without independence; and that of the infatuated Stephens who clung to the idea that Lincoln did not mean what he said, and who now urged "an armistice allowing the States to adjust themselves as suited their interests. If it would be to their interests to reunite, they would do so." The refusal of Lincoln to consider either of these points of view — the refusal so clearly foreseen by Davis — put an end to the career of Stephens. He was "hoist with his own petard."

The news of the failure of the conference was variously received. The *Mercury* rejoiced because there was now no doubt how things stood. Stephens, unwilling to coöperate with the Administration, left the capital and went home to Georgia. At Richmond, though the snow lay thick on the ground, a great public meeting was held on the 6th of February in the precincts of the African Church. Here Davis made an address which has been called his greatest and which produced a profound impression. A wave of enthusiasm swept

over Richmond, and for a moment the President
appeared once more to be master of the situation.
His immense audacity carried the people with him
when, after showing what might be done by more
drastic enforcement of the conscription laws, he
concluded: "Let us then unite our hands and our
hearts, lock our shields together, and we may well
believe that before another summer solstice falls
upon us, it will be the enemy that will be asking us
for conferences and occasions in which to make
known our demands."

CHAPTER XI

AN ATTEMPTED REVOLUTION

ALMOST from the moment when the South had declared its independence voices had been raised in favor of arming the negroes. The rejection of a plan to accomplish this was one of the incidents of Benjamin's tenure of the portfolio of the War Department; but it was not until the early days of 1864, when the forces of Johnston lay encamped at Dalton, Georgia, that the arming of the slaves was seriously discussed by a council of officers. Even then the proposal had its determined champions, though there were others among Johnston's officers who regarded it as "contrary to all true principles of chivalric warfare," and their votes prevailed in the council by a large majority.

From that time forward the question of arming the slaves hung like a heavy cloud over all Confederate thought of the war. It was discussed in the army and at home around troubled firesides.

Letters written from the trenches at Petersburg show that it was debated by the soldiers, and the intense repugnance which the idea inspired in some minds was shown by threats to leave the ranks if the slaves were given arms.

Amid the pressing, obvious issues of 1864, this project hardly appears upon the face of the record until it was alluded to in Davis's message to Congress in November, 1864, and in the annual report of the Secretary of War. The President did not as yet ask for slave soldiers. He did, however, ask for the privilege of buying slaves for government use — not merely hiring them from their owners as had hitherto been done — and for permission, if the Government so desired, to emancipate them at the end of their service. The Secretary of War went farther, however, and advocated negro soldiers, and he too suggested their emancipation at the end of service.

This feeling of the temper of the country, so to speak, produced an immediate response. It drew Rhett from his retirement and inspired a letter in which he took the Government severely to task for designing to remove from state control this matter of fundamental importance. Coinciding with the cry for more troops with which to confront Sherman, the topic of negro soldiers became at once one of the questions of the hour. It helped to focus that violent anti-Davis movement which is the conspicuous event of December, 1864, and January, 1865. Those who believed the President unscrupulous trembled at the thought of putting into his hands a great army of hardy barbarians trained to absolute obedience. The prospect of such a weapon held in one firm hand at Richmond seemed to those opponents of the President a greater menace to their liberties than even the armies of the invaders. It is quite likely that distrust of Davis and dread of the use he might make of such a weapon was increased by a letter from Benjamin to Frederick A. Porcher of Charleston, a supporter of the Government, who had made rash suggestions as to the extraconstitutional power that the Administration might be justified by circumstances in assuming. Benjamin deprecated such suggestions but concluded with the unfortunate remark: "If the Constitution is not to be our guide I would prefer to see it suppressed by a revolution which should declare a dictatorship during the war, after the manner of ancient Rome, leaving to the future the care of reëstablishing firm and regular government."

In the State of Virginia, indeed, the revolutionary suggestions of the President's message and the Secretary's report were promptly taken up and made the basis of a political program, which Governor Smith embodied in his message to the Legislature — a document that will eventually take its place among the most interesting state papers of the Confederacy.   It should be noted that the suggestions thrown out in this way by the Administration to test public feeling involved three distinct questions: Should the slaves be given arms? Should they, if employed as soldiers, be given their freedom?   Should this revolutionary scheme, if accepted at all, be handled by the general Government or left to the several States?   On the last of the three questions the Governor of Virginia was silent; by implication he treated the matter as a concern of the States.   Upon the first and second questions, however, he was explicit and advised arming the slaves.   He then added:

Even if the result were to emancipate our slaves, there is not a man who would not cheerfully put the negro into the Army rather than become a slave himself to our hated and vindictive foe.   It is, then, simply a question of time.   Has the time arrived when this issue is fairly before us? . . .   For my part standing before God and my country, I do not hesitate to say that I would

arm such portion of our able-bodied slave population
as may be necessary, and put them in the field, so as to
have them ready for the spring campaign, even if it
resulted in the freedom of those thus organized. Will I
not employ them to fight the negro force of the enemy?
Aye, the Yankees themselves, who already boast that
they have 200,000 of our slaves in arms against us.
Can we hesitate, can we doubt, when the question is,
whether the enemy shall use our slaves against us or we
use them against him; when the question may be between liberty and independence on the one hand, or
our subjugation and utter ruin on the other?

With their Governor as leader for the Administration, the Virginians found this issue the absorbing topic of the hour. And now the great figure
of Lee takes its rightful place at the very center of
Confederate history, not only military but civil,
for to Lee the Virginia politicians turned for
advice.[1]   In a letter to a State Senator of Virginia
who had asked for a public expression of Lee's

[1] Lee now revealed himself in his previously overlooked capacity
of statesman. Whether his abilities in this respect equaled his abilities
as a soldier need not here be considered; it is said that he himself had
no high opinion of them. However, in the advice which he gave at
this final moment of crisis, he expressed a definite conception of the
articulation of civil forces in such a system as that of the Confederacy.
He held that all initiative upon basal matters should remain with the
separate States, that the function of the general Government was to
administer, not to create conditions, and that the proper power to
constrain the State Legislatures was the flexible, extra-legal power of
public opinion.

views because "a mountain of prejudices, growing out of our ancient modes of regarding the institution of Southern slavery will have to be met and overcome" in order to attain unanimity, Lee discussed both the institution of slavery and the situation of the moment. He plainly intimated that slavery should be placed under state control; and, assuming such control, he considered "the relation of master and slave . . . the best that can exist between the black and white races while intermingled as at present in this country." He went on to show, however, that military necessity now compelled a revolution in sentiment on this subject, and he came at last to this momentous conclusion:

Should the war continue under existing circumstances, the enemy may in course of time penetrate our country and get access to a large part of our negro population. It is his avowed policy to convert the able-bodied men among them into soldiers, and to emancipate all. . . . His progress will thus add to his numbers, and at the same time destroy slavery in a manner most pernicious to the welfare of our people. Their negroes will be used to hold them in subjection, leaving the remaining force of the enemy free to extend his conquest. Whatever may be the effect of our employing negro troops, it cannot be as mischievous as this. If it end in subverting slavery it will be accomplished by ourselves, and we can devise the means of alleviating the evil consequences to both races. I think, therefore, we must decide whether slavery shall be extinguished by our enemies and the slaves be used against us, or use them ourselves at the risk of the effects which may be produced upon our social institutions. . . .

The reasons that induce me to recommend the employment of negro troops at all render the effect of the measures . . . upon slavery immaterial, and in my opinion the best means of securing the efficiency and fidelity of this auxiliary force would be to accompany the measure with a well-digested plan of gradual and general emancipation. As that will be the result of the continuance of the war, and will certainly occur if the enemy succeed, it seems to me most advisable to adopt it at once, and thereby obtain all the benefits that will accrue to our cause. . . .

I can only say in conclusion, that whatever measures are to be adopted should be adopted at once. Every day's delay increases the difficulty. Much time will be required to organize and discipline the men, and action may be deferred until it is too late.

Lee wrote these words on January 11, 1865. At that time a fresh wave of despondency had gone over the South because of Hood's rout at Nashville; Congress was debating intermittently the possible arming of the slaves; and the newspapers were prophesying that the Administration would presently force the issue. It is to be observed that Lee did not advise Virginia to wait for Confederate action. He advocated emancipation by the State. After all, to both Lee and Smith, Virginia was their "country."

During the next sixty days Lee rejected two great opportunities — or, if you will, put aside two great temptations. If tradition is to be trusted, it was during January that Lee refused to play the rôle of Cromwell by declining to intervene directly in general Confederate politics. But there remained open the possibility of his intervention in Virginia politics, and the local crisis was in its own way as momentous as the general crisis. What if Virginia had accepted the views of Lee and insisted upon the immediate arming of the slaves? Virginia, however, did not do so; and Lee, having made public his position, refrained from further participation. Politically speaking, he maintained a splendid isolation at the head of the armies.

Through January and February the Virginia crisis continued undetermined. In this period of fateful hesitation, the "mountains of prejudice" proved too great to be undermined even by the influence of Lee. When at last Virginia enacted a law permitting the arming of her slaves, no provision was made for their manumission.

Long before the passage of this act in Virginia, Congress had become the center of the controversy. Davis had come to the point where no tradition however cherished would stand, in his mind, against the needs of the moment. To reinforce the army in great strength was now his supreme concern, and he saw but one way to do it. As a last resort he was prepared to embrace the bold plan which so many people still regarded with horror and which as late as the previous November he himself had opposed. He would arm the slaves. On February 10, 1865, bills providing for the arming of the slaves were introduced both in the House and in the Senate.

On this issue all the forces both of the Government and the opposition fought their concluding duel in which were involved all the other basal issues that had distracted the country since 1862. Naturally there was a bewildering criss-cross of political motives. There were men who, like Smith and Lee, would go along with the Government on emancipation, provided it was to be carried out by the free will of the States. There were others who preferred subjugation to the arming of the slaves; and among these there were clashings of motive. Then, too, there were those who were willing to arm the slaves but were resolved not to give them their freedom.

The debate brings to the front of the political stage the figure of R. M. T. Hunter. Hitherto his part has not been conspicuous either as Secretary of State or as Senator from Virginia. He now becomes, in the words of Davis, "a chief obstacle" to the passage of the Senate bill which would have authorized a levy of negro troops and provided for their manumission by the War Department with the consent of the State in which they should be at the time of the proposed manumission. After long discussion, this bill was indefinitely postponed. Meanwhile a very different bill had dragged through the House. While it was under debate, another appeal was made to Lee. Barksdale, who came as near as any one to being the leader of the Administration, sought Lee's aid. Again the General urged the enrollment of negro soldiers and their eventual manumission, but added this immensely significant proviso:

I have no doubt that if Congress would authorize their [the negroes'] reception into service, and empower the President to call upon individuals or States for such as they are willing to contribute, with the condition of emancipation to all enrolled, a sufficient number would be forthcoming to enable us to try the experiment [of determining whether the slaves would make good soldiers]. If it proved successful, most of the objections to the measure would disappear, and if individuals still remained unwilling to send their negroes to the army, the force of public opinion in the States would soon bring about such legislation as would remove all obstacles. I think the matter should be left, as far as possible, to the people and to the States, which alone can legislate as the necessities of this particular service may require.

The fact that Congress had before it this advice from Lee explains why all factions accepted a compromise bill, passed on the 9th of March, approved by the President on the 13th of March, and issued to the country in a general order on the 23d of March. It empowered the President to "ask for and accept from the owners of slaves" the service of such number of negroes as he saw fit, and if sufficient number were not offered to "call on each State . . . for her quota of 800,000 troops . . . to be raised from such classes of the population, irrespective of color, in each State as the proper authorities thereof may determine." However, "nothing in this act shall be construed to authorize a change in the relation which the said slaves shall bear toward their owners, except by consent of the owners and of the States in which they may reside and in pursuance of the laws thereof."

The results of this act were negligible. Its failure to offer the slave-soldier his freedom was at once seized upon by critics as evidence of the futility of the course of the Administration. The sneer went round that the negro was to be made to fight for his own captivity. Pollard — whose words, however, must be taken with a grain of salt — has left this account of recruiting under the new act: "Two companies of blacks, organized from some negro vagabonds in Richmond, were allowed to give balls at the Libby Prison and were exhibited in fine fresh uniforms on Capitol Square as decoys to obtain recruits. But the mass of their colored brethren looked on the parade with unenvious eyes, and little boys exhibited the early prejudices of race by pelting the fine uniforms with mud."

Nevertheless both Davis and Lee busied themselves in the endeavor to raise black troops. Governor Smith coöperated with them. And in the mind of the President there was no abandonment of the program of emancipation, which was now his cardinal policy. Soon after the passage of the act, he wrote to Smith: "I am happy to receive your assurance of success [in raising black troops],

as well as your promise to seek legislation to secure
unmistakable freedom to the slave who shall enter
the Army, with a right to return to his old home,
when he shall have been honorably discharged
from military service."

While this final controversy was being fought out
in Congress, the enthusiasm for the Administration had again ebbed. Its recovery of prestige had
run a brief course and was gone, and now in the
midst of the discussion over the negro soldiers' bills,
the opposition once more attacked the Cabinet,
with its old enemy, Benjamin, as the target.
Resolutions were introduced into the Senate declar-
ing that "the retirement of the Honorable Judah
P. Benjamin from the State Department will be
subservient of the public interests"; in the House
resolutions were offered describing his public
utterances as "derogatory to his position as a
high public functionary of the Confederate Government, a reflection on the motives of Congress
as a deliberative body, and an insult to public
opinion."

So Congress wrangled and delayed while the
wave of fire that was Sherman's advance moved
northward through the Carolinas. Columbia had
gone up in smoke while the Senate debated day

after day — fifteen in all — what to do with the compromise bill sent up to it from the House. It was during this period that a new complication appears to have been added to a situation which was already so hopelessly entangled, for this was the time when Governor Magrath made a proposal to Governor Vance for a league within the Confederacy, giving as his chief reason that Virginia's interests were parting company with those of the lower South. The same doubt of the upper South appears at various times in the *Mercury*. And through all the tactics of the opposition runs the constant effort to discredit Davis. The *Mercury* scoffed at the agitation for negro soldiers as a mad attempt on the part of the Administration to remedy its "myriad previous blunders."

In these terrible days, the mind of Davis hardened. He became possessed by a lofty and intolerant confidence, an absolute conviction that, in spite of all appearances, he was on the threshold of success. We may safely ascribe to him in these days that illusory state of mind which has characterized some of the greatest of men in their overstrained, concluding periods. His extraordinary promises in his later messages, a series of vain prophecies beginning with his speech at the African

Church, remind one of Napoleon after Leipzig refusing the Rhine as a boundary. His nerves, too, were all but at the breaking-point. He sent the Senate a scolding message because of its delay in passing the Negro Soldiers' Bill. The Senate answered in a report that was sharply critical of his own course. Shortly afterward Congress adjourned refusing his request for another suspension of the writ of *habeas corpus*.

Davis had hinted at important matters he hoped soon to be able to submit to Congress. What he had in mind was the last, the boldest, stroke of this period of desperation. The policy of emancipation he and Benjamin had accepted without reserve. They had at last perceived, too late, the power of the anti-slavery movement in Europe. Though they had already failed to coerce England through cotton and had been played with and abandoned by Napoleon, they persisted in thinking that there was still a chance for a third chapter in their foreign affairs.

The agitation to arm the slaves, with the promise of freedom, had another motive besides the reinforcement of Lee's army: it was intended to serve as a basis for negotiations with England and France. To that end D. J. Kenner was dispatched to Europe early in 1865. Passing through New York in disguise, he carried word of this revolutionary program to the Confederate commissioners abroad. A conference at Paris was held by Kenner, Mason, and Slidell. Mason, who had gone over to England to sound Palmerston with regard to this last Confederate hope, was received on the 14th of March. On the previous day, Davis had accepted temporary defeat, by signing the compromise bill which omitted emancipation. But as there was no cable operating at the time, Mason was not aware of this rebuff. In his own words, he "urged upon Lord P. that if the President was right in his impression that there was some latent, undisclosed obstacle on the part of Great Britain to recognition, it should be frankly stated, and we might, if in our power to do so, consent to remove it." Palmerston, though his manner was "conciliatory and kind," insisted that there was nothing "underlying" his previous statements, and that he could not, in view of the facts then existing, regard the Confederacy in the light of an independent power. Mason parted from him convinced that "the most ample concessions on our part in the matter referred to would have produced no change in the course determined on by the British Government with regard to recognition." In a subsequent interview with Lord Donoughmore, he was frankly told that the offer of emancipation had come too late.

The dispatch in which Mason reported the attitude of the British Government never reached the Confederate authorities. It was dated the 31st of March. Two days later Richmond was evacuated by the Confederate Government.

CHAPTER XII

THE LAST WORD

THE evacuation of Richmond broke the back of the Confederate defense. Congress had adjourned. The legislative history of the Confederacy was at an end. The executive history still had a few days to run. After destroying great quantities of records, the government officials had packed the remainder on a long train that conveyed the President and what was left of the civil service to Danville. During a few days, Danville was the Confederate capital. There, Davis, still unable to conceive defeat, issued his pathetic last *Address to the People of the Confederate States*. His mind was crystallized. He was no longer capable of judging facts. In as confident tones as ever he promised his people that they should yet prevail; he assured Virginians that even if the Confederate army should withdraw further south the withdrawal would be but temporary, and that "again and again will we return until the baffled and exhausted enemy shall abandon in despair his endless and impossible task of making slaves of a people resolved to be free."

The surrender at Appomattox on April 9, 1865, compelled another migration of the dwindling executive company. General Johnston had not yet surrendered. A conference which he had with the President and the Cabinet at Greensboro ended in giving him permission to negotiate with Sherman. Even then Davis was still bent on keeping up the fight; yet, though he believed that Sherman would reject Johnston's overtures, he was overtaken at Charlotte on his way South by the crushing news of Johnston's surrender. There the executive history of the Confederacy came to an end in a final Cabinet meeting. Davis, still blindly resolute to continue the struggle, was deeply distressed by the determination of his advisers to abandon it. In imminent danger of capture, the President's party made its way to Abbeville, where it broke up, and each member sought safety as best he could. Davis with a few faithful men rode to Irwinsville, Georgia, where, in the early morning of the 10th of May, he was surprised and captured. But the history of the Confederacy was not quite

at an end.   The last gunshots were still to be fired
far away in Texas on the 13th of May.   The surrender of the forces of the Trans-Mississippi on
May 26, 1865, brought the war to a definite conclusion.

There remains one incident of these closing days,
the significance of which was not perceived until
long afterward, when it immediately took its rightful place among the determining events of American history.   The unconquerable spirit of the Army
of Northern Virginia found its last expression in a
proposal which was made to Lee by his officers.
If he would give the word, they would make the
war a duel to the death; it should drag out in relentless guerrilla struggles; and there should be no
pacification of the South until the fighting classes
had been exterminated.   Considering what those
classes were, considering the qualities that could
be handed on to their posterity, one realizes that
this suicide of a whole people, of a noble fighting
people, would have maimed incalculably the America of the future.   But though the heroism of this
proposal of his men to die on their shields had its
stern charm for so brave a man as Lee, he refused
to consider it.   He would not admit that he and his
people had a right thus to extinguish their power

to help mold the future, no matter whether it be the future they desired or not. The result of battle must be accepted. The Southern spirit must not perish, luxuriating blindly in despair, but must find a new form of expression, must become part of the new world that was to be, must look to a new birth under new conditions. In this spirit he issued to his army his last address:

After four years of arduous service, marked by unsur-passed courage and fortitude, the Army of Northern Virginia has been compelled to yield to overwhelming numbers and resources. I need not tell the survivors of so many hard-fought battles, who have remained steadfast to the last, that I have consented to the result from no distrust of them; but feeling that valor and devotion could accomplish nothing that could compen-sate for the loss that would have attended the continua-tion of the contest, I determined to avoid the useless sacrifice of those whose past services have endeared them to their countrymen. . . . I bid you an affec-tionate farewell.

How inevitably one calls to mind, in view of the indomitable valor of Lee's final decision, those great lines from Tennyson:

Tho' much is taken, much abides; and tho'
We are not now that strength which in old days
Moved earth and heaven; that which we are, we are;
One equal temper of heroic hearts,
Made weak by time and fate, but strong in will.

BIBLIOGRAPHICAL NOTE

THERE is no adequate history of the Confederacy. It is rumored that a distinguished scholar has a great work approaching completion. It is also rumored that another scholar, well equipped to do so, will soon bring out a monumental life of Davis. But the fact remains that as yet we lack a comprehensive review of the Confederate episode set in proper perspective. Standard works such as the *History of the United States from the Compromise of 1850*, by J. F. Rhodes (7 vols., 1893–1906), even when otherwise as near a classic as is the work of Mr. Rhodes, treat the Confederacy so externally as to have in this respect little value. The one searching study of the subject, *The Confederate States of America*, by J. C. Schwab (1901), though admirable in its way, is wholly overshadowed by the point of view of the economist. The same is to be said of the article by Professor Schwab in the 11th edition of *The Encyclopædia Britannica*.

Two famous discussions of the episode by participants are: *The Rise and Fall of the Confederate Government*, by the President of the Confederacy (2 vols., 1881), and *A Constitutional View of the Late War Between the States*, by Alexander H. Stephens (2 vols., 1870). Both works, though invaluable to the student, are tinged with controversy, each of the eminent authors aiming to refute the arguments of political antagonists.

The military history of the time has so overshadowed the civil, in the minds of most students, that we are still sadly in need of careful, disinterested studies of the great figures of Confederate civil affairs. *Jefferson Davis*, by William E. Dodd (*American Crisis Biographies*, 1907), is the standard life of the President, superseding older ones. Not so satisfactory in the same series is *Judah P. Benjamin*, by Pierce Butler (1907), and *Alexander H. Stephens*, by Louis Pendleton (1907). Older works which are valuable for the material they contain are: *Memoir of Jefferson Davis*, by his Wife (1890); *The Life and Times of Alexander H. Stephens*, by R. M. Johnston and W. M. Browne (1878); *The Life and Times of William Lowndes Yancey*, by J. W. Du Bose (1892); *The Life, Times, and Speeches of Joseph E. Brown*, by Herbert Fielder (1883); *Public Life and Diplomatic Correspondence of James M. Mason*, by his Daughter (1903); *The Life and Time of C. G. Memminger*, by H. D. Capers (1893). The writings of E. A. Pollard cannot be disregarded, but must be taken as the violent expression of an extreme partizan. They include a *Life of Jefferson Davis* (1869) and *The Lost Cause* (1867). A charming series of essays is *Confederate Portraits*, by Gamaliel Bradford (1914). Among books on special topics that are to be recommended are: *The Diplomatic History of the Southern Confederacy* by J. M. Callahan (1901); *France and the Confederate Navy*, by John Bigelow (1888); and *The Secret Service of the Confederate States in Europe*, by J. D. Bulloch (2 vols., 1884). There is a large number of contemporary accounts of life in the Confederacy. Historians have generally given excessive attention to *A Rebel War Clerk's Diary at the Confederate States Capital*, by J. B. Jones (2 vols., 1866) which has really neither more nor less value than a Richmond newspaper. Conspicuous among writings of this type is the delightful *Diary from Dixie*, by Mrs. Mary B. Chestnut (1905) and *My Diary, North and South*, by W. H. Russell (1862).

The documents of the civil history, so far as they are accessible to the general reader, are to be found in the three volumes forming the fourth series of the *Official Records of the Union and Confederate Armies* (128 vols., 1880–1901); the *Journals of the Congress of the Confederate States* (8 vols., 1904) and *Messages and Papers of the Confederacy*, edited by J. D. Richardson (2 vols., 1905). Four newspapers are of first importance: the famous opposition organs, the Richmond *Examiner* and the Charleston *Mercury*, which should be offset by the two leading organs of the Government, the *Courier* of Charleston and the *Enquirer* of Richmond. The Statutes of the Confederacy have been collected and published; most of them are also to be found in the fourth series of the *Official Records*.

Additional bibliographical references will be found appended to the articles on the *Confederate States of America, Secession*, and *Jefferson Davis*, in *The Encyclopædia Britannica*, 11th edition.

INDEX

Alabama, represented at South Carolina convention, 3; secedes, 7; convention, 8; situation in, 74, 114–20; iron for munitions from, 106; questions of state sovereignty in, 116–19

Alabama, The (ship), 53, 135, 139

Anderson, Major Robert, transfers garrison to Sumter, 6; refuses Beauregard's demands, 15–16; *see also* Sumter

Antietam campaign, 53, 58

Appomattox, surrender at, 201

Arkansas, 14, 74, 112, 113, 114

Arman, shipbuilder of Bordeaux, 132, 133, 135, 140, 143–44

Army, composition and size of, 36–37; state armies, 38, 72; difficulty of enlisting, 76; lack of shoes for, 77–78; desertion, 110, 120, 162, 166; surrenders, 201–02; *see also* Conscription, Military policy.

Ayer, L. M., of South Carolina, 88

Baldwin, of Virginia, tells of martial law, 84

Barksdale, Ethelbert, of Mississippi, 82, 84–85, 192

Beauregard, General P. G. T., and the surrender of Fort Sumter, 15–24; in Georgia, 148, 149

Benjamin, J. P., signs *To Our Constituents*, 3; Attorney-General, 27; Secretary of War, 34, 79 (note); Secretary of State,

34, 40; complaints against, 40, 63–64; life and character, 69–71; denounces Napoleon, 144; on extraconstitutional power, 185; attacked by Congress, 195; accepts policy of emancipation, 197

Blair, F. P., plan of reconciliation, 179–80

Blockade, 51, 56, 77, 105

Bocock, T. S., Speaker of House, 156

Bonds, *see* Finance

Boyce, of South Carolina, argument for peace, 175

Bragg, General Braxton, plan to invade Kentucky, 44; attitude toward press, 59; Davis's confidence in, 69; army conditions under, 96; resigns command, 113–14

Breckinridge, General J. C., Secretary of War, 79 (note)

Brown, J. E., Governor of Georgia, on secession, 5, 6–7; on conscription, 65–66, 75–76; opponent of Administration, 145–49; motives, 174 (note)

Bull Run, Battle of, *see* Manassas

Bullock, Captain James, 135–36

Butler, A. P., of South Carolina, 4

Cabinet, 14–15, 27, 34, 40, 69

Campbell, J. A., Confederate commissioner at Hampton Roads, 180

INDEX

Industries in the South, 105–107

Ismail Pasha, 56–57

Johnson, H. V., 172

Johnston, A. S., 42–43

Johnston, General J. E., 69; succeeds Bragg in command, 114; lower South demands removal of, 128; superseded by Hood, 129; appeals for restoration of, 154, 156; restored to command, 164; surrenders, 201

Johnston, Fort, 17, 20

Kenesaw Mountain, 127

Kenner, D. J., dispatched to Europe, 197–98

Kentucky, 63; plan of Confederacy to win, 44

Labor, 100–02, 152–53

Laird rams controversy, 135–136, 137

Lee, General R. E., inspires army, 43–44; to invade Maryland, 44; and Davis, 68–69; demand of full command for, 154, 156; conspiracy to set up as dictator, 155; made commanding general, 163; opinion of peace project, 180; as statesman, 187–90; officers propose to continue fighting, 202–03; address to army, 203

Lee, Stephen, 18 (note)

Lincoln, Abraham, reëlection, 175, 178; conference at Hampton Roads, 181

Louisiana, 7, 42, 74, 112, 113, 114

McClellan, General G. B., 42, 127

Magrath, A. G., Governor of South Carolina, 152, 153–54, 196

Manassas, Battle of, 33; Second, 43, 59

Mann, A. D., Confederate commissioner at Brussels, 46, 132–133, 142

Martial law, *see Habeas corpus*

Maryland, plan of Confederate States to win, 44

Mason, J. M., capture of, 46; replaces Yancey as commissioner, 47; in England, 52–53, 55, 198–99; in Paris, 137–138, 198

Memminger, C. G., Secretary of Treasury, attempts to establish foreign credit, 48; resigns, 157; *see also* Finance

Mexico, 114; Napoleon III and, 131, 132–33, 134, 138, 139; Confederate negotiations with, 139–40, 144; project condemned by French people, 143; expedition suggested, 179

Military policy, 33, 43–44

Mississippi, represented in South Carolina convention, 3; secedes, 7; typical of new order in South, 29–31; sense of Southern nationality, 31; status of, 74, 114–15

Mobile Bay, capture of, 129

Montgomery (Ala.), general Congress of seceding States at, 9–11

Montgomery Mail, 162

Moultrie, Fort, 6, 20

Munitions, 33, 48, 61, 65, 105–06

Napoleon III, offers mediation, 54, 77; intrigues with Confederacy, 130 *et seq.*; Italian policy, 134, 143; purpose exposed, 142; influence in Mexican policy of the South, 178

New Orleans, loss of, 42, 74

New York Herald, 175

Niter and Mining Bureau supplies powder for South, 106

North Carolina, resolutions concerning Congress of seceding States, 9–10; against secession, 12; secedes, 14; state rights,

Smith, William, Governor of Virginia, 161, 186–87

South, division in, 28 *et seq.*; life in, 99 *et seq.*

South Carolina, convention (1860), 2–4; secedes, 4; community of aristocratic class, 28–29; question of state sovereignty in, 72; political life in, 73–75; anti-Davis, 88; situation in 1864, 150–52; passes State Conscription Act, 151

Southern Advertiser, 117

State sovereignty, 8, 12, 39, 56, 65–66, 71 *et seq.*, 116–18, 169

Stephens, A. H., leads opposition to secession, 7; on state sovereignty, 8; Vice-President in provisional Government, 11; a conservative, 27; elected Vice-President at first regular election, 34; as central figure in South, 172–74; on question of peace, 175–78; commissioner at Hampton Roads conference, 180, 181

Stephens, Linton, 76

Substitutes, Hiring, 92, 103

Sumter, Fort, 6; attack on, 14–23

Taxation, *see* Finance

Tennessee, 14, 74

Texas, secedes, 7; secession issue in, 9; proposes regiment for home defense, 38; last gunshots of war in, 202; *see also* Trans-Mississippi

Thompson, Jacob, 29, 127

To Our Constituents, 2–3

Toombs, Robert, gives information about Fort Pulaski, 6;

a secessionist, 7; Secretary of State, 14, 27, 69; and Sumter, 14–15; candidate for President, 24; leaves Cabinet, 34

Trans-Mississippi, 74, 112, 113, 114

Transportation, 107–08

Tredegar Iron Works, 105

Trenholm, G. A., 157

Vance, Z. B., Governor of North Carolina, on military arrangements, 76–77; seeks to regulate prices, 78; proclamation to urge order, 93–94; urges political changes, 154; reëlection, 170–71; policy, 171–72

Van Dorn, General Earl, 44, 59

Vicksburg (Miss.), 89–90, 96, 112–13

Virginia, and secession, 11–14; calls Peace Convention, 13; political life in, 74–75, 161, 186–87; *see also* Richmond

Voruz, shipbuilder of Nantes, 140

Walker, L. P., 34, 79 (note)

Walker, R. J., 29

Wheeler, Joseph, 118

Winder, J. H., 41

Women, position in Confederacy, 104–05, 110–11

Worth, Jonathan, 93, 169

Yancey, W. L., influence of, 25–26, commissioner to England, 25, 46, 47; relieved by Mason, 47; incident at Havana, 47; attempts to abolish secrecy of Government, 59–60; death, 87